THE PURSUIT OF HAPPINESS

A BOOK OF STUDIES AND STROWINGS

By

Daniel G. Brinton

Paperback: 978-939057539-8

Sanage Publishing House LLP
Mumbai, India

sanagepublishing@gmail.com

One of the founding fathers of modern American anthropology. **Daniel Garrison Brinton** (May 13, 1837 – July 31, 1899) was an American surgeon, historian, archaeologist and ethnologist. He practiced medicine and from 1874 to 1887, edited The Medical and Surgical Reporter, a weekly periodical, in Philadelphia. He also wrote numerous brochures, articles, pamphlets, addresses, and books. Notes on the Floridian Peninsula (1859), The Myths of the New World (1868), American Hero Myths (1882), and The Pursuit of Happiness (1893) are some of his works.

TO THE

HON. GEORGE PIERCE ANDREWS,

JUSTICE OF THE SUPREME COURT OF THE STATE OF NEW YORK,

This Book is Inscribed,

IN MEMORY OF A FRIENDSHIP WHICH HAS CONTINUED UNINTERRUPTED SINCE OUR EARLIEST COLLEGE DAYS.

"We hold these truths to be self-evident,—that all men are created equal; that they are endowed by their Creator with certain inalienable rights; that among these are life, liberty, and THE PURSUIT OF HAPPINESS."—*The Declaration of Independence of the United States of America.*

"The sun and stars that float in the open air,

The apple-shaped earth and we upon it, surely the drift of them is something grand,

I do not know what it is except that it is something grand, and that it is Happiness."

—Walt Whitman.

CONTENTS

PART I.

Happiness as the Aim of Life.

I. Is a Guide to Happiness Possible? And, if Possible, is it Desirable?

The pursuit of happiness,—the pursuit of one's own happiness,—is it a vain quest? and, if not vain, is it a worthy object of life?

There have been plenty to condemn it on both grounds. They have said that the endeavor is hopeless; that to study the art of being happy is like studying the art of making gold, which is the only art by which gold can never be made. Nothing, they add, is so unpropitious to happiness as the very effort to attain it.

They go farther. "Let life," they proclaim, "have a larger purpose than enjoyment." They quote the mighty Plato, when he demands that the right aim of living shall stand apart, and out of all relation to pleasure or pain. They declare that the theory of happiness as an end is the most dangerous of all in modern sociology—the tap-root of the worst weeds in the political theories of the day, for the reason that the individual pursuit of enjoyment is necessarily destructive of that of society at large. Moreover, they urge, who dares write of it? For he who has not enjoyed it, cannot speak wisely of it; and in him who has attained it, 'twere insolence to boast of it.

Over against these stands another school, not, by any means, solely a modern school. If that boasts Plato as its leader, this can claim Aristotle as its master. It is with the single aim to become happier, said that wise teacher, that we deliberately perform any act of our lives. This is the final end of every conscious action of man. That alone is the true purpose of existence, which, by itself, and not as a means to something else, makes life worth living and desirable for its own sake; and happiness—happiness alone—fulfills this requirement.

Through the ages this conflict has continued. We find the thoughtful Pascal declaring that every free act of the will has, and can have, no other end in view than the increase of the individual happiness, be it so seemingly inconsistent as drowning or hanging oneself; while the distinctively modern school of social philosophers, without any exception, pin to their banners the maxim of their master, Jeremy Bentham, "The common end of every person's efforts is happiness;" and they love to confound the ascetics by proclaiming, with Spencer, that "Without pleasure there is no good in life;" or asserting, with Ward, that the sole aim of a right sociology is the organization of happiness. Nay, they have gone so far as to project a series of sciences by which the human race is to reach a condition of entire enjoyment. They give us "Eudæmonics," or the art of the attainment of well-being; "Hedonism," or the theory of the securing of pleasure; and even the "Hedonical Calculus," by which we can to a nicety calculate how much any object, if secured, will add to our felicity.

These excellent authorities have therefore answered the inquiry whether the pursuit of happiness is a possible occupation, by showing that in fact we cannot of our own wills do anything else; and though we often pursue it blindly and by false routes, we can, by taking thought and learning of others, follow it up successfully. So also taught Aristotle, who tells us in his *Ethics*, "It is possible for every man by certain studies and appropriate care to reach a condition of happiness."

Since the aim of enjoyment is thus natural, even thus necessary, to man, since it is the motive of his every action, how important that it should be guided by the dictates of wisdom, and not condemned and discarded as evil! Have not those who declared it criminal smothered the germ which they should have nursed?

Away with the cold and cruel doctrines which for ages have darkened the lives of men by teaching them that enjoyment is folly and pleasure a sin! If the reasoned pursuit of happiness conflicts with current morality, so much the worse for that morality. Away with it, and in the light of a younger day seek a better one. What is right is reasonable, and what is reasonable is right. Enjoy yourself; it is the highest wisdom. Diffuse enjoyment; it is the loftiest virtue. Not only are the two compatible; they are inseparable; as the sage Rasselas said to the Princess: "It is our business to consider what beings like us may perform; each laboring for his own happiness by promoting within his circle, however narrow, the happiness of others."

All agree that we should strive for the happiness of others; it has even been said that this is the only moral justification of any act of our lives. But the cup which we are to proffer to all, we are, forsooth, forbidden to taste ourselves! What is good for everybody else is bad for oneself!

There is something radically wrong here, both in fact and logic. Mental moods are contagious, and the man who enjoys little will prove a kill-joy to others. Who are more disagreeable than those Philistines and Pharisees who insist on making you happy against your will, and contrary to your inclinations? I have noticed that the usual pretext for annoying people is solicitude about their welfare. But, as a rule, people are not happy whose pleasures are assigned them by others. Nobody's vegetables are so sweet as those from my own garden, and if the whole world set to work to please me, I am sure I should be discontented. These moralists put the cart before the horse. Before we are qualified to make others happy we must compass happiness in some degree for ourselves; and our success with others will be just to that degree and no more. The quality and intensity of enjoyment which we ourselves have is alone that which we are able to impart to others. To assert, therefore, that we should make no effort to obtain or increase this, is as illogical as can be.

Here some one may think I am caught in my own trap. For if people cannot assign pleasures to others, is it not an impertinence to offer instruction on the subject? Can anybody tell me better than myself what I like and what I desire?

True, but the difference is wide between telling me what things should please me, and telling me how I can best please myself; and the latter is the aim of right instruction in this matter. That it is badly needed, one who runs may read. Most people pursue unhappiness more steadily than happiness. Only fools find life an easy thing; to the wise it is a perpetual surprise that they get along at all. To them, life is a lesson to be learned, and happiness is a science the first axiom in which is to seek knowledge. To be happy one must work for it, and not merely have the wish and possess the requisites; as Aristotle so prettily expresses it, "As at the Olympic games, it is not the strongest or handsomest who gain the crown, but only those who join in the combat."

There is boundless need for a clear statement of the true theory of personal happiness. It has been neglected, misconceived, and decried long enough, and countless lives have been darkened in consequence. Such a theory, to be true, must be applicable to all men, of all sorts and conditions, because the desire of happiness is the common motive of all. Has it yet been discovered? That is the object of the present inquiry—for it is little more than an inquiry; but be sure that when it is discovered and set forth, it will come not as something new or strange, but like some half-forgotten, long familiar truth.

Not only, therefore, is it desirable, it is the bounden duty of every man to consider his own highest happiness, to learn what that is, and to go to work to secure it. It is his duty to his neighbors as well as to himself; more than that, it is his first duty to his kind. It is incumbent on every generation to transmit an increased store of social and personal felicity to posterity. This is the only good reason for the continuance of the race. But a generation does nothing except through its individual members; hence, it all comes back to the personal effort for happiness.

But the moralist will object, Is not this doctrine one of absolute egotism, of stark selfishness?

This objection is what has nullified and cast into disfavor every essay ever written, from the Nichomachean Ethics downward, which attempted a reasoned and practical art of increasing personal happiness. They have all been frowned down as selfish and, therefore, immoral.

It is time for this opposition to cease. It rests on a misunderstanding of terms, on a confusion of different sensations, on the bad books of some writers, but mostly on ancient prejudice and an ignorance of facts. Let the subject be approached with a mind free from bias; let the false beacons hung out by some schools be disregarded; above all, let a clear understanding of what happiness consists in be gained; and this potent objection will be dismissed from the case.

Let us turn, then, to the definition of happiness.

II. The Definition of Happiness.

In science a definition is not a resting-place, but a stepping-stone. It is needless, therefore, to call the catalogue of obsolete and obscure definitions of happiness. Some, indeed, say that the definition, like the thing itself, is still unfound.

I do not think this is so. Between the physiologists and the psychologists, I believe we are in a position to explain what happiness is; and if in parts the explanation is a trifle subtle, it is not really obscure.

Happiness is not the same as pleasure, but it is generally built upon or grows out of pleasurable feelings. We must begin, therefore, our analysis with these, and with their opposites—the painful feelings.

Pleasure and pain are both ultimate and undefinable experiences of the mind. We cannot resolve them further; but we can note certain unfailing relations they bear to the organism, which explain their significance.

Pleasure characterizes the normal and unimpeded exercise of physiological functions of all kinds. There are as many elementary pleasures as there are sensations. Pain is present only in the reverse conditions. Modern physiologists have established, therefore, the fundamental law, that pleasure connects itself with vital energy, pain with its opposite; in which they have not gone beyond, even if they have caught up to, the maxim of Spinoza: "Pleasure is an affection whereby the mind passes to a greater perfection; pain is an affection whereby it passes to a lesser perfection."

Such is the meaning of pleasure or of pleasurable feelings; and there is no lack of writers, and weighty ones, too, who maintain that happiness is merely the excess of pleasure over pain; or the utmost pleasure we are capable of; or the aggregate of continued pleasurable feelings. All such phrases are wide of the mark. They confound distinct things, and ignore the boundaries between the different realms of mental action.

We must leave the physiologists and turn to profound analysts of purely mental action, such as Hume and Kant, for the right understanding of the meaning of happiness. For these, its inseparable factors, are the Will and Self-consciousness. As Kant expresses it,—"The Desire of Happiness is the general title for all subjective motives of the Will." Desire is really stimulated, not by the image of past pleasure, as Locke and his followers teach, but by the conception of Self. The satisfaction of desire is not merely such, but is the satisfaction of the Self, in thus reaching a greater perfection, to use Spinoza's phrase. Only by discriminating the object from the Self can the pleasure of the subject become an end in itself. Hence the real aim of the pleasure-seeker, though he is rarely intellectually conscious of it, is to feel his own Self, his own being, more keenly. Aristotle expressed this when he wrote,—"Pleasure is the feeling which accompanies Self-realization."

To the extent, therefore, that pleasure develops the sense of Self-consciousness it partakes of a higher nature than mere sensation, which man shares in common with the brutes; and to that extent it can claim the name of Happiness, a feeling inseparable from free will and conscious individuality. In man a true pleasure must always be a pleasure in something else than the pleasure itself; that is, it must heighten the sense of personal existence.

It is only the conception of Self as a permanent subject to be pleased, that stimulates man to fresh endeavors, that makes him seek knowledge and freedom, that lifts him above the beast, contented with the satisfaction of its appetites. This is what Fichte meant when he said that the consciousness of Self alone enables us to understand life and enjoy it. Nothing is truer than the motto, "*Être heureux, c'est vivre,*"—to be happy is to live.

Here, again, some uneasy moralist will point the finger and raise the cry of "selfishness." It is time to have done with this purblind, this high-gravel-blind moralist, who refuses to distinguish between self-feeling and self-seeking. There are two self-loves. The one is inseparable from personal existence, the necessary point of departure of every conscious action, whose activity and whose end are alike in the object outside of the self; the other is that egoism which directs both the action and its end toward itself. The former is fecund, ennobling, inspiring; the latter is sterile and enfeebling. Rightly understood, nothing is so admirable as self-love; but love yourself, not for what you are, but for what you may be. The wisest of teachers set no higher mark for duty than, "Love thy neighbor *as thyself.*" It was a modern and unphilosophical derogation which substituted for it, "*Vivre pour autrui.*" In living the best for ourselves, we live the best for others.

The conclusion which we have now arrived at, that happiness is the increasing consciousness of Self, leads us to reflect whether this mental state is brought about solely by what is generally known as "pleasures," or whether some other feeling, not usually classed as such, may not have the same effect. Man can enjoy only through action, and all his happiness depends on action; but there may be a great deal and very intense activity in spheres of experience to which the terms pleasure and pain, in their physiological sense, do not apply. Indeed, such activities may be present along with physical pain and mental suffering, and yet the law hold good:

that if these are of a nature to exalt the consciousness of self, they may be a well-spring of happiness under circumstances the most unfavorable. This explains a passage of Epictetus which I thought over a long time before I mastered its significance,—"Happiness is an *equivalent* for all troublesome things;" not that it excludes or abolishes them, but that it is a compensation for them. This puts the whole art of happiness in a different light. It may teach us to avoid some pains and troubles, and this is well; but the best of it will ever be to give us an *equivalent* for the many that remain. Any text-book of felicity which leaves this out of account may as well be burned by Monsieur de Paris.

Now we can understand what Plato meant when he said that the right aim of living should stand out of relation to pleasure or pain. He had in mind these other activities which give in some natures an intenser sense to self-consciousness than any mere nerve reaction. The ancient ideal was the greatness of the individual, the richness of his imagination, the reach of his intellect, the strength of his will, the firmness of his friendship, the devotion of his patriotism, the singleness of his life and purpose in some noble aim. This it was that floated before the intellectual vision of Plato and led him to scorn the pleasures of the sense and the charms of tranquillity.

Let us applaud him; for we moderns are not ignorant of the luxury of toil and the joy of strong endeavor; we too, like Othello, "do agnize an alacrity for hardness;" with Seneca we can say, "*Res severa est verum gaudium.*" But we hold it needless and unwise to leave any sunny field uncultured on whose soil may be trained to bloom the fragrant flower of pleasure.

The yearning for joy is a cry of nature which can never be stifled. Give heed to it and obey it. It calls you to wider horizons, to warmer sympathies, to a fuller growth, to a completer development. It holds the secret of Evolution. It is the incessant prompter to a higher form of existence. Biologists have discovered that the avoidance of painful and the search for pleasurable sensations are the first principles of organic animal life, and are those which have developed the amœba into the man. In him, this general consciousness has blossomed into Self-consciousness, and to this he owes all the growth of his higher nature, his essentially human powers. To the extent that this is brought into harmony with the sum of his faculties and with his surroundings, he wins that something greater than pleasure which we call happiness. From the culture of this, if from any source, he must look for the advent of those new spirit-powers which more fortunate generations in the hereafter may enjoy. Who knows but those, our dear children of after days, may gain a still higher form of consciousness, one through which they will be brought into harmony with the perfect working of the Cosmos, and the ancient fable be realized, of men who walked the earth as gods?

III. The Relative Value of Pleasures.

The learned have established what they call "a hierarchy of the sciences," a scheme which shows the relative value and scope of the various departments of knowledge, and how the one rises upon the other. So in the Science of Happiness there is a series of degrees, a *gradus ad gaudium*, which measures the relative value of human enjoyments and the dependence of the higher upon the lower.

The ignorance or the disregard of this fact has led to the ruin of more individual lives, and to more fatal misfortunes to the race, than any other error whatsoever. The poison of all false religions and philosophies lies either in condemning pleasure or in commending low forms of it; and the one is as hurtful as the other. The religion which to-day numbers more believers than any other, Buddhism, aims its loftiest aspirations to the extinction of all desire and the abolition of all enjoyment. These are the words of Buddha himself:—

> "Let no man look for what is pleasant; for not to find it is pain.
>
> "Let no man love anything; for the loss of the beloved is sorrow.
>
> "After pleasure follows grief, and from affection comes fear.

> "I have run through many births, and painful it is to be born again and again; but now, O Thou Builder of this house, Thou hast been seen, and not again shalt Thou rebuild it. The mind has attained to the extinction of all desire."

This is the ideal of happiness that four hundred millions of human beings hold before their minds to-day. If there is any truth in the modern philosophy which teaches that pleasure lies in functional activity, no more pernicious message could be commended to mankind than that which Buddha brought.

He is far from the only preacher of such a gospel. "To rest in peace," "to sleep in the Lord,"—is not this the religious hope and aspiration of millions of Christians? It is not a whit higher than the Nirvana of the Buddhist.

The avoidance of pain is the lowest form of happiness; more correctly, it is its mere negative, and scarcely deserves to rank as one of its grades. Yet, alas! to how many millions is it the highest form imagined! To how many is the only escape from unhappiness to forget themselves! This is the cause of that thirst for intoxicants and narcotics which undermines and infects modern society. Dr. Johnson would still find the multitude agree with him in his opinion, that a man is never happy except when he is drunk!

Those Quietists who preach tranquillity and contentment as the goal which all should seek are but one step higher. Indifference to pleasure, or a reduction of the number of pleasures, is a sign of weakening of the reason and of a retrogression in development. No man has a right to be happy because he is contented; though he may well be contented because he is happy. To be "void of strong desire," set free from hope and fear, snugly harbored from all storms of feeling, so far from being the condition of the sage, is the aspiration of the fool. Keen sensations awaken the sentiments, emotions fertilize the intellect, passions educate the reason. The brute goes through life without a smile or a tear; man's proud privilege is to weep and to laugh.

The ancients taught that philosophical happiness is to want little, and that it is the error of the vulgar to want much and to enjoy many things. The truer doctrine is that happiness is expansion and growth, the enriching of our natures by manifold experiences, and the securing this by the multiplication of our desires. The avoidance of pain and the limitation of our hopes to our powers are sometimes valuable preliminaries to the pursuit of happiness, but are not always essential to it, and in many instances an over-solicitude about them destroys all chance for a higher felicity. Happiness does not come of itself. It has to be worked for, fought for; and courage and endurance are as necessary in this as in any other struggle. In the path of every pilgrim to the Celestial City stand from time to time the giant figures of Death and Pain, and shake their spears, saying, "Wilt thou dare?"

The sources of pleasure should, therefore, be multiplied to the utmost, and they should be classified, so that undue value should not be assigned any one class. Theoretically, there is nothing troublesome about this; practically, it is often an insurmountable difficulty. The pleasures of the senses are inferior to those of the emotions, and these in turn are ranked by the enjoyments which pertain to the exercise of the intellectual powers. No one of these can wholly exclude the others. They are all inseparably united in the individual entity; but the individual can enjoy only with the faculties he possesses, and in proportion to their relative strength. It is as absurd to ask more of him, as it were to invite the gouty to a foot race, or the blind to admire the colors in a painting.

It is well to establish and to recognize this hierarchy of enjoyments, beginning with those of the sensations common to animal life everywhere and culminating in those of pure reason, whose crowning felicity is the pursuit of truth; it has been done, and well done, by many writers; but what has been generally overlooked is that this scheme can have small practical application to the conduct of life if it is not fully recognized that no one of these roads to happiness can be successfully pursued while the others are neglected, or branded with the sign, "Entrance forbidden."

This is where Asceticism has committed its fatal blunder, and for thousands of years has made miserable the lives of millions. Instead of self-control, it has demanded self-abnegation; instead of the due and proportioned exercise of all the powers, it has ordered the absolute disuse of some of them; quite as often of the highest as of the lowest, of reason as often as lust. Under this baleful doctrine nations have become misshapen in mind, atrophied in culture, distorted from honest nature's rule, mean, miserable, and inefficient. Yet this same doctrine is preached to-day from thousands of pulpits in lands of highest civilization. Is it not time for the common sense of most to rise in protest against such a survival from the Dark Ages of the life of the race? Reason blushes only for pleasures which she cannot explain, and he who acquaints himself with the whole nature of man knows that all his powers and faculties have their appropriate use. The ascetic may claim a happiness all his own; but so do the extravagant and the vicious; both stand condemned before the results of their own successes.

The intellect has no right to chide the enjoyments of the senses. Pleasures differ in degree and permanence, but not in kind. *As pleasures* they are on a par, whether derived from objects of sense, from the emotions, or from the understanding. Such analysts of mind as Kant and Epictetus agree that there is no *essential* distinction between the most refined and the coarsest gratifications. "It is one and the same vital force expressing itself in the Desires, which is affected by all objects which cause Pleasure."

IV. The Distribution of Happiness.

Having reached an understanding about what happiness means, and some notion as to its various grades, it will next be worth while to study its distribution in the several classes of society, in contrasting grades of civilization, in the two sexes, and at various ages. This will be dealing with the subject according to the methods of natural science, and it ought to lead to some interesting conclusions.

One might expect to find a general agreement as to the main facts. Far from it. The common belief is that happiness increases with the means, or at least with the capacity, for happiness. It is this belief which inspires men to labor for the means and improve their capacities. But the philosophers nowise concede its correctness. Hume argued that all who are happy are equally happy; and Paley maintained that happiness is about equally distributed among all orders of the community; that the plowman gets as much real enjoyment out of life as the philosopher, and the beggar at the gate as much as the monarch on the throne. To which Dr. Johnson replied that a small glass and a large one might be equally full, but the latter holds more. The capacity, he justly argued, of the philosopher to receive a multiplicity of agreeable impressions is greater than that of the peasant, and therefore, other things being equal, the quantity of his enjoyment will be greater.

The learned Doctor, indeed, sometimes insisted that felicity increases directly with the means of enjoyment. Representing the latter by money, he would say that a man with six thousand pounds a year should be ten times as happy as the one with six hundred a year; and if he is not, it is because he is an ass.

Here he was certainly wrong. Some of the main elements of ordinary happiness are in the possession of every class of society, high and low, poor and rich; such as the means of self-preservation, family ties, friendship, amusement, and repose. What wealth and power add to this common stock becomes less and less at each remove. This consideration led Bentham to question whether the prince is twice as happy as the laborer, and to doubt whether ten thousand times the wealth brings with it twice the enjoyment. His followers have attempted to frame the relation in a mathematical formula, and have expressed it in the maxim, "The rate of increase of pleasure decreases as its means increase."

The conclusion is a satisfactory one for several reasons, and appears to be borne out by the experience of mankind. Gibbon quotes the saying of the potent Sultan Abderrahman, who at the close of his brilliant reign of forty years asserted that during the whole of that time he had had but fourteen days of happiness; on which the historian comments that he himself could claim many more than the famous Prince.

The moral of the story is, that it is not the multiplication of the *means*, but of the *sources* of pleasure which is the secret of happiness.

The extremes of the social conditions are almost equally unfavorable, the one through the privations it entails, the other through the burdens it imposes and the distractions it brings. Both are unpropitious to self-culture, and this alone lays substantial foundations for a considerable enjoyment of life.

A similar debate has taken place in reference to the distribution of happiness in the different grades of civilization. Rousseau and his followers never tired of portraying the delights of the savage state. Like the ancient Greeks, he placed the Golden Age in some Arcadia of untutored shepherds and lawless huntsmen. It is the fashion to smile at his notion as the vagary of a crank; but the scientist of our own day whose studies of the conditions of savage tribes stand ahead of all others, has deliberately expressed almost the same opinion as the result of his long researches. "Civilization," writes Dr. Theodore Waitz, "has proved itself impotent to increase the sum of human enjoyment."

What a sad conclusion to reach! And what a comment on the jubilant shouts of those optimistic philosophers who have been telling us how vastly better off we are than any of our ancestors!

Yet these also are right in a certain sense. The most careless reader of history must hug himself for joy to think of the multitude of miseries and oppressions which have disappeared from society in the last few centuries. The inquisition, slavery, trial by torture, the press gang, are but a few of them. At that time the fate and the happiness of the individual were in the hands of priests and kings and nobles; now, thank Heaven! in most countries, especially in our own, they are chiefly in the control of the individual himself.

Nevertheless, it is quite possible in a given state of society that general evils may diminish while personal suffering increases, owing to an undue exaltation of sensitiveness, a sort of moral hyperesthesia, together with the multiplication of desires beyond the means of satisfying them. This is, in fact, the condition of modern society; and these traits, together with its instability and rapid changes, and the bitter competition instigated by its enlarged freedom, have unquestionably very greatly diminished the amount of happiness which might have been expected from the ameliorations of the last few centuries.

There is but one remedy which will be of permanent avail, and that is to educate the individual into some other ideal of happiness than that which is filled by the acquisition of property or the gratification of the senses. The main purpose of all social institutions which have been created up to the present time has been the getting and the keeping of property; the motive of the higher civilization which is to come will be the preparation of the race for a life which will be filled and sustained by its intellectual and spiritual contents.

The Greek philosopher thanked the gods especially for two blessings,—that they had created him a Greek and not a barbarian, and a man and not a woman. Evidently he held strongly to the opinion that in his own country, at least, the men had the better part in life.

Though woman held an honorable position in Greek society, it was inferior to what she enjoys in the United States to-day; yet the philosopher, were he among us, would probably repeat his thanks. It is quite certain that in the distribution of happiness the stronger sex has seized the lion's share.

To be sure, there are certain advantages in the struggle for life which a woman seems to be conceded, and others which she by nature possesses. She is less exposed to dangers than men; she escapes avocations of the greatest hardship and risk; she is generally supported by the labor of others, and she is allowed privileges in many small matters of daily life which are denied the other sex. Of her own nature she is less the slave of passion, less reckless, less of an egotist, less inclined to deeds of violence and crime. In all civilized countries the convictions of women for criminal offenses are less than one-third those of men.

These points are in favor of her securing a larger share of happiness; but they are checked by many and serious countervails. She is born an invalid. Her periodic sickness, the burden of pregnancy, the pains of childbed, the years of distress at her climacteric age, place her for the best part of her life at a fearful disadvantage. Enter the library of a physician and turn the leaves of his thick volumes on obstetrics and the diseases of women if you would have your sympathies harrowed by a long list of dreadful maladies of which men know nothing.

Another thought disables a woman, and must lessen and darken the enjoyment of her life in every rank and condition of society. Unless under immediate protection, she is always exposed to the possibility of insult and assault, and no general safeguards will ever entirely remove this danger.

Outside of these inevitable disabilities, the unfortunate elements in the modern condition of women are owing to the legal and religious tyranny of men. The dogmas of Christianity distinctly lowered her position compared to what it was in the Roman Republic or the cities of Etruria. At Delphi, the thoughts of the gods found expression through the mouth of the priestess; but the founder of Christian institutions forbade women to speak in the churches. The ancient Greek prayed to the goddesses, Minerva, Aphrodite, and Demeter, as the givers of the good things of life, of wisdom, of love, and the fruits of the field; but to the Christian, evil and death and pain were what the first mother of the race brought as a dower to her husband and left as a legacy to her children.

These pernicious teachings led to a steady oppression of woman in all ages of Christianity, our own included. So thoroughly did they become ingrained in the minds of men that the most liberal scarcely recognized their presence. The priest laid on the bride the obligation of obedience to her husband; and the philosopher, Rousseau, servile in this to the ideas of his time, when he has completed the education of his Emile, contents himself with saying to Sophie, "This is the man whom it is your duty *to endeavor to please*!" Not until a man arose emancipated from all tradition, did the teaching of Plato that the sexes should be socially and politically equal find a modern philosopher to echo it; that was when John Stuart Mill wrote his essay on the freedom of woman; though it would be unfair to the growth of religious thought not to add that he had been anticipated in most practical points by the despised dissenter, George Fox. Only when the spirit of teachers such as these will have permeated the institutions, the religions, and the social traditions of the day, will women have a fair chance with men at the common stock of happiness possible for the race.

Most fatal of all measures to the happiness of woman has been the unceasing effort of ecclesiasticism to make marriage, for her, an indissoluble sacrament of servitude, instead of an equal civil contract, in which no obligation is assumed on the one side which is not as fully accepted on the other. Mill well remarks that the miseries produced in the lives of individual women by subjection to individual men are simply incalculable. Guarantee the wife every right and every privilege that the husband has, and the increased happiness of both will be sure to crown the concession.

The remedy for this state of things is the proper education of girls and women. But it is a remedy not likely to be administered soon, in spite of the talk about it. Men prefer ignorance in women, as women admire blind devotion in men; because these enable each sex to cheat the other more easily. Nothing is more essential to her happiness than that she should be taught the hygiene of her sex early in life; but the popular voice says ignorance means innocence, and thousands of women are condemned to life-long misery in consequence. I had a medical friend who wrote a volume of excellent advice to mothers, and his profession almost ostracized him for it. Beyond all things, a girl's education should be directed toward manual training and exercises of the understanding; instead of that, she is taught the fine arts and regaled with poetry and fiction. Her imagination is fostered by lectures on esthetics, and her memory crammed with moral platitudes which have no place in real life; while the principles of business and the maintenance of her own rights are left out of her training. I cannot but attribute to this the most common and fatal defect of the female mind,—its lack of the sense of abstract justice.

Men are so selfish and ignorant that they do not understand how much they themselves forfeit by thus reducing the position of woman. In my studies of ethnology, I first inquire the position occupied by woman in a given tribe or nation; for I have discovered no better common measure of civilization. The profoundest thinkers of the age have recognized the principle here involved. Goethe closes the second part of Faust—which is a poetic presentation of the evolution of European culture—with the significant words,—"The forever feminine leads us onward." His friend, Wilhelm von Humboldt, expressed a double fact in the phrase,—"The Woman stands nearer the ideal of Humanity than the Man; but she more rarely attains it." She does not, because she is prevented by prejudice, by dogmas, and by laws. Until these weeds are scorched to ashes by the growing flame of free intelligence, neither will she secure the meed of happiness which is her due, nor will man have found the right road to his best prosperity.

Plato proposed to banish poets from his ideal Republic because they are such liars. The prevalent notion that childhood and youth are the happiest periods of life is largely owing to this mendacious crew. I have rarely met an intelligent person of years who held the opinion. It arises from forgetfulness of early sorrows, from false pictures of youthful joys, and from undue attention to present pains. Most of those who really feel such regret are the moral or literal prodigals, who have wasted their substance in riotous living, and bewail, not the lost happiness, but their inability to repeat their follies.

The rule of honest nature is that enjoyment should steadily increase up to the full maturity of the powers, mental and physical. This, under favorable circumstances, is between forty-five and fifty years of age. After that, physical decadence sets in, and only by exceptional strength or by increased effort can its fatal progress be for a while stayed. From inquiry of many persons, I am persuaded that the rule of the increase of enjoyment up to this turning-point is on the average correct.

That old age is synonymous with wisdom is a comical deception which the graybeards have palmed off on the world, because by laws and customs they hold most of the property, and want most of the power as well. In fact, diminution of the physical powers means decay all round. "As we grow old," observes Thoreau, "we cease to obey our finer instincts." It is an error to talk of the accumulated wisdom of years. The experience of youth serves but to lead old age astray; and this is seen nowhere so plainly as when an old man pretends a zest for the pleasures of the young. "No fool like an old fool" is the proverb. Such men are "out of their class," as a trainer of athletes would say. Every age has pleasures sufficient, which are appropriate to it, and these alone should be sought for. To those who know and respect these laws of nature, old age is very tolerable. It brings many compensations for its inevitable losses; and though not likely to be so happy as the best of middle life, it should be and often is superior in this respect to youth. Probably it would generally be so were it more willing to learn the lessons appropriate [Pg 36]to it. Bonstetten goes so far as to say, "No one can be happy till he is past sixty;" but the proverb of the ancient Rabbis holds forever good,—"He who teacheth the old, is like one who writes on blotted paper."

V. Principles of a Self-Education for the Promotion of One's Own Happiness.

The purpose of this chapter is not to enter into practical details of an education for happiness—that is the mission of the rest of the book,—but to establish certain general theoretical principles on which such an education must be carried out in order to be successful.

And first, I must repeat what I have already intimated, that any permanent and even moderate stock of happiness does not fall into the open mouth, like the roasted quails in the fairy story, but can be obtained only by methodical pursuit and constant watchfulness. Eternal vigilance is said to be the price of liberty; and liberty is only one of the necessary elements of happiness. Meditation, forethought, and the formation of a clearly defined Plan of Life are all required, and even then success is far from certain.

At the outset, I must attack as unsound a maxim which has been assiduously disseminated by the school of economists of which Herbert Spencer is the leader. It is put in the form,—"The greatest efficiency is the greatest happiness." It would be a calamity if this were true. The pursuit of happiness would be hopelessly circumscribed, as but few in the world can attain maximum efficiency in anything. Fortunately, it is historically false. Those men who have won fame by their enormous personal capacity have certainly not been the happiest of their kind. Far from it. They have been men of one idea, absorbed by some "ruling passion," to which they have sacrificed all else, and consequently, so far from gaining happiness, have usually ended by wrecking their own and others'. It is not the reach of a man's abilities, but the use he makes of them, that decides his fortune. Spencer's maxim is precisely the reverse of the principle which should govern an education intended to secure the utmost enjoyment for the individual and those around him. Such an education should not be concentrated on one faculty of the mind nor on one subject of study, but should extend in all directions, be broad and many-sided. It is an education within the reach of every one, which requires no schoolmaster but oneself; and yet confers a degree on its graduates more valuable than any university can bestow.

Its leading theoretical principles may be grouped under five propositions:—

I. The multiplication of the sources of pleasure and the diminution of those of pain.

II. The maintenance of a high sensibility to pleasurable impressions.

III. The search for novelty and variety of impressions.

IV. The establishment of a proper relation between desires and pleasures.

V. The subjection of all pleasures to the increase of happiness.

These principles are not speculative or doctrinal, but are based on the physiology of the nervous system and the constitution of the human mind.

I. Let us begin with the first, for it is the basis of the whole Art of Pleasure. Differently expressed, it means that the sum of our enjoyment must be enlarged by increasing our sources of enjoyment. In other words, we must set to work to acquire tastes in addition to those which we already have by nature or previous education. The most useful instruction is that which teaches us to profit by all our chances. People are never so unhappy as they think they are, because at the moment they forget how many sources of pleasure remain for them.

Review the field. Take an "account of stock." Most people have five senses in tolerably good order. How many have seriously calculated the number of different gratifications each of these senses is capable of yielding? Beyond these lie the inviting fields of the Agreeable Emotions, whose prolific soil needs but to be stirred to teem with flower and fruit; and still beyond, but in easy reach, the uplands of Reason and Thought rise into the purer air, and offer perspectives of entrancing beauty.

All these resources are, to some extent, open to every one. But most sit like a peasant at the table of a prince, refusing to taste the choice viands which are before him, because he cares only for the beans and hodge-podge of his daily fare.

Along with the multiplication of the sources of enjoyment must go the studied avoidance of profitless pain. I say *profitless* pain, because there is pain which is profitable, and to avoid that would be to miss the best of life, as I shall try to show on a later page,—a distinction too often forgotten by those political economists who are preparing the race for the era of universal happiness.

All pain is profitless which is incurred by a deliberate violation of natural law, such as needless neglect of health or disregard of social custom. When we confess that we have "made fools of ourselves," we suffer what our knowledge could have prevented, and we recognize it. The part of wisdom is to avoid such suffering.

Here lies the incalculable value of knowledge in this pursuit. I do not mean extensive learning or erudition, but knowledge of ourselves, of our immediate natural surroundings, and of our own sphere of probable activity. The chief value of Knowledge, says Epictetus, is that it destroys Fear. We do not dread the known, but the unknown. Its worth does not stop there. It enables us to escape disasters, to lessen pain, to mitigate suffering in ourselves and others, and to secure many joys. Three verbs, observes the philosophical Littré, express the ideal perfection of human happiness—to know, to love, and to serve.

The true end of what is called "culture," or a "liberal education," is not to store the mind with a variety of facts useful in managing men or in making money, but to expand our sympathies, to bring us in touch with all that is beautiful and enjoyable in our lives; it is to increase the sensitiveness of our finer instincts, so that they will respond more readily to the delicate stimuli of pleasurable impressions. Thoreau, walking behind the farmer's cart, claimed to have stolen the best part of the load of apples when he inhaled the fragrant aroma from the fruit. To him it was more gratifying than to have filled his stomach with the acid pippins.

Of all false maxims for happiness, that to be "content with little" is the falsest. We should want immensely, but want wisely. To supply such wants there is no need of the revenue of a kingdom or the lore of a pedagogue. Not one man in a thousand exhausts the means of wise enjoyment which are daily within the reach of his hand. Why go far a-field to seek the treasure buried neath his own hearth-stone? What he needs is to study himself and his environment, so as to protect himself from the dangers to which he is exposed, and to draw from such circumstances as he is placed in, and from such faculties as he is possessed of, the maximum of gratification which they can render him. If all persons acted consistently on this principle, the general sum of human happiness would be indefinitely increased.

The kind of knowledge which is most serviceable to this end is by no means difficult to acquire. It falls within the range of a common school education, and ought to be made a part of it, with the definite aim of promoting personal happiness. Professor Alexander Bain, who belongs to the Scotch common-sense school of philosophers, and who treats all questions in a business-like manner, has drawn up a scheme of such an education, which any one can carry out for himself. It is so excellent that I present its main features, with amplifications of my own.

a. A Knowledge of the Bodily Constitution.

This means an acquaintance with the outlines of anatomy and physiology, the rules of personal and general hygiene, some understanding of the most prevalent diseases in the locality in which we live and those to which we are individually most liable, and the simplest means for their prevention and treatment; what best to do in cases of sudden accidents and emergencies; and last, though not least, the precepts for training, strengthening, and beautifying the body and the features.

b. The Elements of the principal Physical and Chemical Sciences.

Even a rudimentary knowledge of the sciences of chemistry, geology, geography, astronomy, of mechanics, steam, electricity, etc., such as can be acquired from primary text-books, increases wonderfully our interest in the world around us and in what we see and hear every day of our lives, and thus furnishes a thousand sources of enjoyment, besides being certain to find numerous practical applications of utility.

c. The Study of the Mind.

This is at once a delightful pastime and an indispensable art for success in many lines of business. It means an acquaintance with the motives which actuate men in their decisions, the personal traits which make up their characters, their passions and their ambitions, their weaknesses and their prejudices. Men distinguished for what is called "executive ability," statesmen, diplomatists, promoters and managers of great enterprises, all either possess by nature or have acquired by study this insight, and to it they owe their success. To some degree, all can attain it by observation of those around them, and by the perusal of works which explain the constitution of the mind and the dominant motives of human action. To this should be added an unprejudiced reading of modern politics and history, especially of one's own country and State.

d. A Knowledge of the Principles of Business.

Worry about business affairs is probably the commonest cause of unhappiness. A great deal of it is inevitable; but a large share of it would be prevented were both sexes taught early in life the general rules and customs of business, and those principles of financial management, investment, prudence, and economy, which are nearly as fixed in their operation as those of the motions of the stars. There are many popular handbooks on this subject, and one such ought to be in every household.

e. A Study of the Value of Evidence.

A remarkable writer, De Senancour, who under the name of Obermann composed some strange books early in this century, maintained that if men would tell the truth and could predict the weather, nearly all the sufferings which afflict humanity would disappear. There is a great deal in his opinion. At present, all men have a rooted aversion to truth, and neither wish to tell it nor to hear it beyond a strictly limited amount. But as a knowledge of facts is essential to right action, the estimation of evidence and the calculation of probabilities are necessary to a prosperous life. A man who has this faculty is said to be gifted with "sound judgment," but it is quite as much an acquirement as a gift. There are well-known principles by which the value of testimony is balanced and the weight of evidence decided. They are in daily application in our courts, and can be applied at least as successfully to affairs outside.

Such are the outlines of an education directed toward increasing the sources of enjoyment and diminishing the causes of suffering; and what remains to be said is little more than an extension of the principles thus laid down.

II. The second principle is the maintenance of a high sensibility to pleasurable impressions.

To reach the right meaning of this we must begin with physiology. All impressions of the nervous system, that is to say, all feelings, may be compared or studied with reference to three criteria, their Quality, their Intensity, and heir Persistence. Feelings of the same quality, as a rule, heighten each other's intensity, but persistence is usually inversely to intensity. The keener the sensation, the shorter its duration. The story is told of a French scholar who, for suspected heresy, was subjected to judicial torture on the rack. When the instrument was extended the first time, dislocating several of his joints, he uttered a cry of agony; but at the second extension he burst into laughter. "At my own ignorance," he explained, "to suppose that I could feel such suffering twice."

It is essential to anything like a constant flow of pleasurable feelings that we maintain a high state of vigor in the organs of sensibility; and this can only be accomplished by a careful limitation of intensity in favor of persistence of feeling. Occasional nervous impressions of a very high degree of intensity are not only consistent with health, but increase it; but their frequent repetition, and especially the determined effort to maintain them for long periods, inevitably result in a deadening of the sensibility and a lack of response to ordinary and healthful stimuli.

The ignorance or disregard of these physiological laws explains some of the most disastrous and conspicuous failures to attain happiness where every circumstance seems propitious. The neglect of them is the origin of that morbid condition of the mind which has been called "the disease of the century," *la maladie de la siècle*,—Ennui.

The bitter pessimist, Schopenhauer, delighted to show the worthlessness of life, whose only variety is from the toil of pursuit to the ennui of possession; while the sweet mystic, Pascal, discovering in the same feeling the greatest misery of man, saw in it that which would prove his salvation, for it would lead him to renounce the vanities of the world and give himself unto God. The one opinion is worth as much as the other.

If we make an anatomy of Ennui, as Burton made an anatomy of Melancholy, we shall find that two different, though allied, mental conditions have been grouped under the name.

The one is that sense of immeasurable boredom which we feel when placed in uncongenial conditions, especially such as ought to be welcome to us, as listening to good advice, or hearing instructive lectures, or reading useful books,—like this one. We are driven to any revolt by such inflictions. The scholar will turn gypsy and the virtuous youth a vagrant to escape them. As a boy, at stiff company dinners, I used to suffer from a keen desire to throw a plate through the window, or commit some other outrageous breach of decorum.

What is the meaning of this innate revolt against conventionalism and formality and respectability? The divines are ready to tell you that it is a clear case of original sin. It is nothing of the kind. It is the inherited and unquenchable thirst for freedom in the human heart, and in some temperaments the strength of this passion for liberty is such that any sacrifice is cheap to purchase it.

> Perhaps these have not the worst of the bargain. "Who is the happiest man in France?" some one asked the academician, D'Alembert. Quelque misérable, "Some wretched fellow," he replied. There is infinite philosophy in his answer. Browning, in *Fifine at the Fair*, discusses the question with amazing insight into human motive. He demands—
>
> "What compensating joy, unknown and infinite,

Turns lawlessness to law, makes destitution—wealth,

Vice—virtue, and disease of mind and body—health?"

He finds the answer in the "frenzy to be free" which is the ruling passion in such characters as he describes. He is right, for ennui of this kind is unknown in conditions of the largest personal freedom, as in the savage state and among the vagabonds of society.

The other form of ennui arises not from external conditions, but from those which are within. It is a species of dissatisfaction with self. A man is generally his own stupidest companion. According to the proverb, "Poor company is better than none;" because the poorest of all is oneself. A curious paradox that has been noted is that the more a man thinks about himself, the less he cares to be alone with himself! We no longer shun solitude from the dread of bandits or ghosts, but to escape the sight of the specters which arise within ourselves. How many of us can boast of the "sessions of sweet silent thought" which the poet praises as the crown of felicity? Amid the gay throng of pleasure-seekers at Ranelagh, Dr. Johnson felt himself distressed by the reflection, "That there was not one in all that brilliant circle who was not afraid to go home and think."

There is a moral virtue which the Roman philosophers called *sufficientia* and the Germans *Selbstgenügsamkeit,* which terms are not at all translated by the English "self-sufficiency." Let the word go; the thing is what is needed. Make yourself an agreeable companion to yourself, and this form of ennui will be known to you no longer. This can only be accomplished by the constant and well-directed exercise of your personal activities, and by the maintenance of a high degree of sensibility to pleasurable impressions.

III. The search for novelty and variety of impressions.

The Art of Happiness prescribes that instead of cultivating a limited number of pleasurable impressions up to a high degree of intensity, we should seek a large variety, diverse in quality, moderate in intensity, considerable in persistence. This precept, properly understood, is consistent not only with a high, but perhaps with the highest degree of gratification, for it is supported by another physiological law of the greatest interest. This is, that the utmost zest of pleasure is invariably conditioned on the entire novelty of the sensation. This fact is so familiar that it is embalmed in common proverbs, as that "Variety is the spice of life," and the like. But the deep significance and the manifold applications of these sayings are rarely considered.

Entire novelties are within the reach of few, and come of themselves but seldom. Fortunately, their agreeable effect can be closely imitated by influences quite within our own control; that is, by the remission and alternation of the pleasures already our own. This alone will maintain the efficacy of any pleasure, for it is a sad fact that in impressions on the nervous system, persistence can never become permanence. Remission and reaction in all sensations are demanded by that eternal and infinite law of Periodicity, or Rhythmical Recurrence, which is the last and highest in the Universe of mind or matter. This in turn enforces on us the importance of aiming for a multiplicity of sources of pleasure, so that we may heighten their impressions by frequent variety.

Here again we come into conflict with that cherished delusion which makes contentment and tranquillity the chief elements of happiness. With political economists, it often arises from a confusion of the spheres of the State and the Individual. The State properly aims at peace, established order, routine, and material ends; but the Individual should seek variety and activity, he should try untrodden paths and risk unknown crises. This alone will make him a many-sided, strong character, responsive up to the full measure of his powers to all impressions of natural enjoyment.

The foe he has to guard against in this joyous quest is Habit. This is the tyrant whose iron scepter enslaves most men. The promptings of pleasure and pain are far from being the only incentives; probably they are by no means the most numerous or potent. The "ruling motives" of most persons are simply the associations, customs, ideas, and aims with which they have been longest in contact. A given mental tendency soon becomes predominant, its easy yoke becomes adjusted to the neck, and the man pursues his way in life without more resistance than the ox to the wain. Vain the attempt to break his fetters and sever the bonds of his habits. He is satisfied to reply, as the Arab to the visitor, who would teach him a better agriculture--"Thus did my father before me and thus my mother taught me; and in this manner shall I continue."

All attempts to make men happier on a large scale have been shattered against the rock of this stubborn conservatism. Only at rare intervals has it been riven by the shock of some mighty emotion which has swept, tornado-like, over the soul of a nation, uprooting the tangled growths of bigotry and routine. The only hope is that here and there an individual will arise and say to himself, "I shall believe nothing merely because those around me believe it; I shall do nothing merely because I am accustomed to do it; I shall render to myself a reason for my every decision and act."

If some one asks, Why this invective against Habit, easy Habit, soft as a padded chair, comfortable as an old shoe? the answer must come from an analysis of mind. I have before shown that all true motives of the Will are directed toward the avoidance of pain or the attainment of pleasure. These alone are clearly conscious motives, distinguishing between Self and Object, and therefore heightening to the sense of individual life. Whatever we do "by habit," on the other hand, we do, in a greater or less degree, by what physiologists call "unconscious cerebration," and through the involuntary action of our nervous and muscular systems. This automatic action of our organism is constantly encroaching on our consciousness, submerging it, like the tide the shore; darkening it, like the night the landscape; swallowing it inch by inch, like the boa his prey. The struggle against Habit, therefore, and all that Habit means, prejudice, bias, bigotry, authority, is a struggle for life, and the nation, the society, the individual, who succumbs in the contest is, by the very fact, bound hand and foot and cast into utter darkness.

IV. The establishment of a proper proportion between desire and pleasure.

Through the mouth of Hamlet Shakespeare makes the philosophical reflection—"There is nothing either good or bad but *thinking* makes it so;" in other words, the value of anything reckoned in the currency of enjoyment, lies not in the thing itself but in the strength of our wish for it. Most of the aims of effort are like curios, whose price is gauged entirely by the anxiety of the amateur to obtain them, and not by any intrinsic quality.

In life there is no more useful faculty than to be able to put the right price on pleasures. The best of prudential maxims is "Count the cost." The outlay of effort should be in a just relation to the return which can be reasonably reckoned upon. A given pleasure should be sought with an energy strictly in proportion to the gratification which it can actually yield,—not in proportion to a false ideal of that gratification as portrayed by the exaggerations of passion or morbid desire. When infatuation or fascination or an over-heated imagination leads the chase, horse and rider will be soon landed in the ditch. Pain and disappointment ever follow an end sought in excess of its real value. Again to quote the great dramatist, the "expense of passion" is sure to be succeeded by "a waste of shame."

The precept of education which is thus enforced is the regulation of desire by reflection and deliberation. Proceed to an appraisement, as in business affairs. Ask yourself the grounds of your desire. Is it from experience, or merely on hearsay, and from a groundless imagining of what the object might yield if attained? If it is from experience, and the tasted sweet whets anew the appetite, recall the reaction and the consequences, and if they were unpleasant, present them fully before the bar of your judgment. If imagination alone influences you, remember that you are playing the children's game of "swapping in the dark," and are liable to exchange solid value for dross. "Depraved affections," observes Lord Bacon, "are false valuations."

V. The last of the five principles stated is the crown of all of them,—Make all pleasures a part of happiness.

I have already explained the difference between mere pleasurable sensation and happiness in the true sense of the term. While the former belongs to man's animal nature, the latter is intimately associated with the consciousness of Self. The power of discriminating one's Self from the rest of the universe, and making one's Self the subject of one's own observation is a faculty peculiar to man alone. There is nothing which lends him more potent aid to accomplish this than his pleasurable sensations. This alone imparts to them any real value in the history of the individual or the race, and through this their value becomes inestimable.

This has always been recognized as true of some of them; but the error of most teachers has been that they have refused to acknowledge the value of all pleasure to this end, the excellence of all enjoyment, when it is brought into relation to the full nature of man. Some have claimed that the charms derived from the esthetic and benevolent emotions are enough to fill our lives; others advocate intellectual joys; many preach that the religious sentiment offers all that man needs; while counselors of an opposite tendency cry, "Eat, drink, and be merry, for to-morrow ye die."

All are wrong. The spirit of sound culture will recognize the whole nature of man and the solidarity of all his parts, and will insist on respecting that unity, if his true development is to be accomplished. For this reason it will strive to render the pleasures of the senses and emotions as intellectual as possible; and with not less earnestness will aim to keep the pleasures of the intellect in touch with the emotions and the senses. Its principle will be that the more intimately the gratifications of sense are infused with emotion and thought, the more they will be both purified and strengthened; and the closer the web into which we can weave the austere joys of the reason along with the emotions and the feelings, the more sympathetic, wide-reaching, and ennobling will those joys become. As the ancient mason mingled water from the sky with clay from the earth to make the bricks wherewith to build the temple, so the permanent structure of human progress can be erected only by combining in due proportion the extremes of man's delights.

A real though mysterious bond unites sense with that which is above and beyond sense. Toward this Unknown it is ever striving, though blindly and unconsciously. In lower forms of life this has led to that marvelous series of transformations which, at last, have reached their culmination in man. In him the struggle no longer expends itself in physical changes, but frames the ideals which float before his mind, constantly spurring him to attempt the impossible. Rest assured that the analogy which holds good throughout all organic nature fails not in him, its most perfect production. Somehow, by unknown ways and under the guidance of unseen laws, his unwearying effort to discover the invisible in the visible, the permanent in the transient, the ideal in the real, will infallibly lead him in triumph to the final goal of all Life. Whenever, without ulterior aim and for its own sake, we give ourselves up to the admiration of some grand scene in nature or masterful production of human art, we feel and recognize how near to us, how much a part of us, is that invisible and ideal world in which are set up the goals of man's noblest aspirations. To unite these opposites, to illuminate the pleasures of sense with the light of the ideal, and, on the other hand, to capture its evanescent rays by entangling them in material enjoyments, is the final precept of the Art of Happiness.

Anthropology, the Science of Man, is the point of convergence of all the other sciences; and the one aim of the Science of Man is the Happiness of man; thus the Pursuit of Happiness is the end of all pursuits. Pope displayed the inspiration of the poet when he devoted the final epistle of the Essay on Man to a discussion of,

"Happiness, our being's end and aim."

The study of Philosophy, said Socrates, is the studying how to die. I add, that the study of Happiness is the studying how to live; and that he who acquires either, possesses both.

Rules for happiness are worth studying, even if they are no better than the rules for writing poetry: which are said to prevent ill poets, if they never make good ones.

Fortunately, happiness is a tree with many roots. It does not depend entirely on outward circumstances; nor entirely on temperament or health; nor entirely on ourselves or on others; nor entirely on prudence or study. By cultivating any one of these, the tree will bear some fruit. So bounteous are the gifts of nature, that if we simply reduce the evils of life to something manageable, our happiness will often take care of itself.

All history teaches that those who renounce pleasure for themselves are least scrupulous about inflicting pain on others.

Genuine pleasure has this unique trait: the more you get for yourself, the more you provide for others.

Pleasure and pain are common to all animals; and man's most exalted joys and sorrows bear a family likeness to these universal sensations.

In a certain sense, every pleasure is a victory, every pain a defeat; the former is allied to movements of attack, the latter to those of defense or submission.

Pains are pains to all; while there are many pleasures which are such to but a few; though there is no reason but ignorance why they are not shared by the many.

The bliss of ignorance consists in not knowing how much we never had, and in living unaware of the worst of our mistakes.

Spiritualize your senses; the lowest of them may become first in the kingdom of culture. Sensualize your intellect; only thus can you attain the companionship of those noble brethren, Humanity and Urbanity.

Our happiest moments are those in which we believe we can realize our ideals.

Those who condemn the pursuit of Happiness reveal the baseness of their own conception of it.

The doctrine that we should get rid of our wants by extinguishing our desires is suited to the clown in the story, who cut off his ears because they were cold.

Self-realization is widely different from self-manifestation.

An error that persuades us we are happy is more welcome than a truth which shows us we are not.

Life is a sphere with an infinite number of sides; but, like the terrestrial globe, to each individual it seems a plain, bounded by his own horizon, with himself in its center.

PART II.

How far our Happiness depends on Nature and Fate.

I. Our Bodily and Mental Constitutions.

To live happily, we must in the first place *live*. Transparent truism, but how often forgotten! How many of our pleasures tend to weaken life, rather than to strengthen and to lengthen it!

Some philosophers have found the sense of existence a sufficient synonym for happiness. Sir William Hamilton expressed this opinion with perhaps an ambiguous under-meaning when he said,—"To lead a happy life is to live all the days of one's life;" but Dr. Johnson, moralizing on the learned pig, expanded the idea more clearly when he maintained that the mere prolongation of existence is a sufficient compensation for a very considerable amount of suffering. We see the correctness of his observation in the multitude of examples of those who cherish their years when poverty, old age, and disease would seem to have robbed them of all value. When nothing else is left but life, life alone becomes worth all else.

Self-preservation, therefore, which means the care of life and health, is the first and a necessary condition of personal happiness. But what a task is this!

When the child wakes to consciousness and surveys the scene around him, he finds himself on a battle-field divided between two mighty combatants in unremitting conflict—Necessity and Chance, the laws of Nature and the caprices of Accident. Not even the gods, said the ancient Greeks, can struggle with Fate and Fortune, those elemental powers, Anangke and Tyke. What is man that he dare venture the fray?

Each individual is scarcely more than a volume of quotations from the works of his ancestors, selected with little appropriateness to the Essay on Life which he has himself to compose. Mysterious and unrecorded influences extending over untold generations have combined to make him what he is, and to endow him with a personality which he can never escape from, nor transcend. The boy, the man, can no more run away from his parents than he can from himself. He may renounce and cast out the traits which he has inherited, but he cannot get rid of them. Unbidden and unnoticed, they will slink back and abide with him forever. They are not his servants, but belong to his family, his clan, his race. He can change or dismiss them no easier than he can the color of his skin or the shape of his skull.

These are the laws of Heredity. They bind the individual as with a tether to an immovable stake. But the tether is not a fetter. It allows him a certain freedom, so that within the limits of those laws he can wonderfully modify himself and better his fortunes. More than that, he can "cozen the gods," and outwit both Fate and Fortune, if he sets about it right. And how is that? By learning the laws of his own nature and of the physical surroundings which environ him. Knowing them, he can turn them to his own advantage.

Let us see what these are; and first, those which concern the bodily and mental constitution of the individual, so far as they bear upon his happiness in life.

Those who have studied this subject, physicians and physiologists, draw a twofold distinction in the traits of the individual, discriminating between those which he has by birth, and those which can be traced to incidents in his own history after birth. Of the former, some are "hereditary," that is, traceable with reasonable surety to his ancestors; and others "congenital," meaning those which appear to be due to incidents in his own history before birth. To this latter curious class belongs the development of what anatomists call "monsters;" and there are thousands such in the moral world from allied causes, of whom the anatomist takes no heed, the whole complexion of whose lives has been changed by some light impression at this infinitely susceptible period.

Of hereditary traits, the most salient are those which stamp on the individual his racial and ethnic characteristics. He is a white man or a negro, a Mongolian or an American Indian; he is, within these limits, a Jew or a Greek, a Chinaman or a Japanese; each with his own features, color of skin, straight or crisp hair, and all the other marks, mental and physical, which belong to his particular race and people. Each one of these will help or handicap him in the pursuit of happiness.

Less prominent, but yet indefinitely potent, are those characteristics which he inherits from his family or clan, and from his immediate parents. To these he generally owes his stature, his physical strength, his symmetry and beauty, or his lack of these, his constitutional diseases, his longevity, and his language,—all mighty agents in turning the kaleidoscopic pictures of his future life. From this source he probably also derives that which physicians call his "temperament," which is in many instances the trait which decides on his general happiness or unhappiness in life; for it is often observed that a particular temperament descends for generations in the same family.

The "congenital" peculiarities are those which especially mark the individual. Sex is one of these. Physiologists now know that the human individual commences of the neuter gender, and that the decision as to whether it shall be masculine or feminine is an incident, or more justly an accident, of its later life. Certain diseases, malformations, and bodily marks are also congenital, as well as those slight variations of the form and features which make up the physical personality; and more than all, to the obscure and momentous period when the spirit is folded in the womb does the individual owe his strongest tastes and inclinations, his talents, and, when he possesses it, the divine endowment of genius. Therefore the physicians of ancient times established the maxim,—"*Ingenium est ingenitum*."

With this miscellaneous stock of heirlooms, with this farrago of festering rags and family jewels, poisoned fangs of serpents and fragments of holy crosses, ancient formulas of withering curses and saintly blessings whispered by a thousand generations of ancestors, the babe is born into the world. His one duty in life is to battle with these unseen but fateful influences, to defend his freedom against their subtle approaches, to master their armories, and to maintain and develop ever more and more his own separate individuality, utilizing his inherited powers and tendencies or destroying them, as they make for or against his own true happiness.

To accomplish this, he will call to his aid such powerful allies as education, self-training, personal hygiene, the establishment of desirable habits, and the assistance of trusty friends. By such aids he can modify his own nature, and Fate cannot wholly prevail against him. He will realize the meaning of the noble words of Buddha, the Awakened,—"Self is the Lord of Self; who else should be the Lord?"

Let us see in some detail what he has to contend with, and how he should set about it.

Nature is equitable. The more inflexible her laws, the wider the liberty they allow; the stronger the rivets of her chains, the longer they are. Thus it is that racial peculiarities, though the most indelible of all, do not stand in the way of man's enjoyment. They do indeed limit the quality, but probably not the quantity, of pleasure in life. The race which anatomists consider the lowest, the African negroes, is famous for its gayety and buoyant spirits. Danger, poverty, even slavery, do not quench their cheery, care-free disposition. The majority of them are like Hamlet's friend, Horatio, with naught but their good spirits to feed and clothe them. Little reck they of the future. Music and song, talk and laughter, are all they want to fill their days.

How different the American Indian! not that he is the solemn and taciturn savage whom the romance-writers depict. In his native state he is light-hearted, too; but there is one poison a single drop of which embitters all his cup of joy, the poison of restriction. Lessen his liberty ever so little, and all light is shut out of his days. Everywhere the race is the same. Its surroundings count as nothing. In the long Arctic night the Eskimo is blithe and carolsome, far from the approach of the white man; while amid the glorious scenery and Eden-like climate of Central America, the native languages have a dozen words for pain and misery and sorrow for one with any cheerful signification.

The white race has a greater range and a higher quality in sensation and emotion than any other. Modern psychologists—who are in fact physiologists—have demonstrated this by experiments. The white race alone responds to the most delicate stimuli in art, in religion, and in scientific thought; and probably its members alone are, as a race, capable of the highest degrees of happiness; though single individuals of the other races doubtless may equal them in this respect.

Let the individual of any race not despair of joy. Let him pursue it with a firm intent and a clear understanding of what it is, and he will surely receive it to the capacity of which his nature is capable. The barriers of race or nation fence him off from no flowery fields or sun-lit pastures. There are gates, if he will seek them, which open on them all.

More ominous to his welfare are the traits he inherits from his own family, his immediate ancestors. How true it is that a man's worst enemies may be those of his own household! How dreadful it is that they may be those who love him most, who brought him into the world, who would die for him! As in Ibsen's terrible drama, the ghosts of the follies of our fathers may ever hover near us, poisoning our blood, darkening our daylight, blighting our lives, transmitting to us the seeds of insanity, the mortal leaven of consumption, or the loathsome virus sucked from the breasts of illicit pleasure. Who can deliver us from the body of this death?

No one but ourselves. Here more than elsewhere it is vain to sit by the wayside and cry to the passers-by for aid. Scant is the consolation and slight the assistance they can proffer us. We must ourselves search the arid plains for such meagre roses and shriveled leaves as remain for us to twine the chaplets of pleasure. He who is born to an inheritance of disease—and the majority are—should boldly recognize it as his special danger, and should study the means of its prevention. If of the serious character of those I have mentioned, he should make it his main business to escape its inroads by choosing an appropriate avocation, by removal to other surroundings, and by adopting a course of life which medical science prescribes as that most likely to postpone indefinitely its outbreak. There are thousands of such wise men in every civilized community, who were born with these blood-taints, but who successfully escape them,—till they fall a victim to some other malady. Nor have these by any means the worst part of life. The habit of constant watchfulness and forethought thus engendered is one of the most valuable guarantees of personal happiness; this is why among confirmed and chronic invalids we often meet a degree of cheerfulness and even gayety which surprises us.

These beings are doubly fortunate; for they have escaped not only their particular malady, but another not less dangerous to their own well-being and that of those around them—a morbid valetudinarianism, a perpetual fussiness about their own ills and ails. The victims of this complaint are the *malades imaginaires,* constantly coddling themselves, thinking of no one but themselves, of whom we meet an endless number in the wealthier classes of society. It must have been of such as these that old Dr. Johnson blurted out his rough judgment,—"Every sick man is a scoundrel!" They usually forfeit more than they win by such selfish concentration. It is a symptom of disease to think constantly about one's health. The most effectual remedy for it is to think about increasing the comfort of others.

There is no need for me to go into details of what such a training should be to protect one as much as possible against the development of hereditary diseases. The precepts must be adapted to the particular case and circumstances, and in this age Personal Hygiene is a science by itself, with abundant and competent instructors. Its scope is not limited to the prevention of disease, but extends to the strengthening and symmetrical development of the whole body. No one who intelligently pursues his happiness will omit the study and practice of its precepts. Health is not indispensable to happiness. Fortunately, no one condition is indispensable. But there is no other condition which so generally and potently contributes to it. Therefore, he who intelligently seeks enjoyment will pay early and frequent attention to athletic culture; he wil seek some healthful and agreeable physical exercise; his posture will be erect and his breathing full; his periods of effort will be prolonged to positive fatigue, and will be judiciously alternated by others of changed activity or complete repose.

The trainer of athletes lays down for his pupils a rigid discipline. He is as far from encouraging overstrain and excessive exercise as he is indolence. He condemns stimulants and narcotics beyond a most moderate use; and he is solicitous about such things as sleep, and food, and cleanliness. If his pupils find it repays them to submit to his stringent dicta for the hope of winning a champion's belt or a silver medal, is it not worth while to accept the much less severe regimen necessary to obtain the Olympian garland woven of the joys which a sound and elastic health offers?

All that I have said on this subject applies with even greater force to girls and women than it does to youths and men. Women, alas, as I have before remarked, have the worser part in life. No one but a physician sees how much of their wretchedness is owing to ignorance or neglect of the laws of physical health. There is no excuse for this in this day. The wicked old doctrine which taught that ignorance of their own nature is a necessary condition of innocence in girls ought long since to have been cast out of window. It is as false as that the seclusion of a harem is necessary to insure the virtue of wives. In nine cases out of ten a woman's health in life depends on the care she exercises between early puberty and the birth of her first child; and this is the precise period when the prejudices of society strive to keep her in profoundest ignorance of the laws which govern her own bodily functions!

More delightful to any true woman than the pleasures of health or the praise of her faculties is the adoration compelled by her beauty. Madame de Stael regretted that she could not exchange her magnificent powers and her literary fame for the personal charms of Madame Recamier. She was right. Let no woman be persuaded to abate one jot or tittle in her cult and culture of the comely in face and form. Only cramped bigots and dull pedants cheapen the value of beauty.

Beauty is real; it is that which alone is permanent and visible; it lurks behind a thousand masks and distorted countenances, ever struggling to body itself forth; it is the manifestation of potent and mysterious natural laws, which but for it would remain forever hidden from us. Its proud power is to awaken Love with all her joyous train; and Love means the unconscious attraction of the Ideal, the noblest incitement to human endeavor.

These are not mere phrases. They are facts proved by the life-history of the human race. As nations advance in civilization from the savage condition to one of enlightenment, their ideals of physical beauty steadily near a definite and the same conception of the perfect human form, the underlying motive of which is the highest function and a perfected capacity. This progress is rapid in proportion as hat which is peculiarly human in man is cultivated beyond that which is merely animal. Not that any rigid canon of proportion or mechanical norm will ever be attained; because the endeavor is toward the Ideal, and this is beyond the reach of mortals.

These are the teachings of the learned in the Science of Man; they are constantly supported by the experience of history. Beauty is and ever has been the Desire of all Nations. For it, in all time, men have counted as nought their honor, their gold, and their hopes of heaven. For it, they have poured their heart's blood on a thousand stricken fields, and laughed at death and hell. Think you that the noblest of the race would have thus reckoned the world well lost, and paid all that, wisdom holds precious for a smile from the lips of loveliness, were there not some strange and wondrous compensation, some immortal and unearthly significance, in Beauty itself?

There is such significance, and nowhere is it so visible as in the perfect female face and form. This is the most beautiful of all objects in nature or art. To it we turn to gaze, forgetting the works of the greatest masters which may be spread before us; unmindful of the sublimest scenes which mountain and lake may combine to show us. Nearer than anything else does it bring us to that Ideal World whose margin forever recedes as we approach it; louder in its presence sound the tinkling bells of that Fairyland which guards the fruition of our sweetest hopes and dreams.

The beauty of woman has been the incentive of physical progress in the race and the inspiration of its noblest arts. It shadows forth the embodied ideal of humanity, and in its resistless strength binds men as slaves to its chariot. But does it confer happiness on the possessor? Sad and faithful is the reply of the poet—

> "In every land
>
> I saw, wherever light illumineth,
>
> Beauty and Anguish walking hand in hand
>
> The downward slope to death."

La fatale donna di bellezza, "the fatal gift of beauty," says the proverb of the Italians. Perilous is the path of mortals who walk too near the gods. The brightest beacons are those which most attract the foul birds of night. The men or the women who shine beyond their fellows through the bounteous gifts of nature are the chosen targets for envy and hatred and calumny and all their ugly crew. In the clash of violent emotions excited by the radiance of fair faces, in the contention of love and jealousy, despair and passion, it is rare that the cause of it all escapes scot free. Her wisdom is also weakened by the adoration she receives; she assumes that it is for herself, forgetful that a passing disease or the accident of a moment may rob her of her charms forever. She has yet to learn that those alone are worthy of admiration to whom it is not a necessity.

Thus it happens that the *vis superba formæ,* the "proud strength of beauty," so often proves a fatal weakness to its possessor. American women who have followed the fortunes of generations of belles tell me that those distinguished for their physical charms have as a rule met with less success and less happiness in their after life than their plainer sisters. This is not as it should be. Regularity of features, mobility of expression, harmony of coloring, symmetry of form, and gracefulness of motion are the five sides of the mystic pentagram of beauty, and, like that of the ancient astrologers, it should have power to exorcise and banish all evil spirits, and constrain men and demons to the willing service of ennobling joys.

A beautiful woman is the nearest approach we have to the perfected ideal of humanity in general. When in their statues of Apollo, Adonis, and the Hellenized Antinous, the ancient Greek sculptors portrayed their highest conception of manly beauty, in many points they approximated the male to the female form, recognizing in the lines of the latter a superior artistic excellence and the consummate expression of the ideal of the beautiful; nay, even the embodiment of the supreme of intellectual gifts. "Something feminine," observed Coleridge in his Table Talk, "is discoverable in the countenances of all men of genius." Therefore the artists represent angels as of that age when the male is most similar to the female,—*tra giovane e fanciullo,* between youth and childhood, as Tasso describes the archangel Gabriel.

Great is the value of physical culture; but let there be no misunderstanding as to what this value is. Such culture, under whatever title it appears, is but a means to an end. They miss its meaning who make it an end in itself. Its sole worth is to aid in bringing about that mental condition or process which we term felicity, or joyousness.

This point is more easily carried in some constitutions than in others. Much depends on what is called the "temperament," and so much has been written about temperaments that I cannot afford to omit a reference to them. To be sure, they do not fill so many pages in modern writings as in those of an earlier age; but this may be because they are not now so well marked as they once were. Functions, like fashions, are subject to the law of periodicity.

The four leading temperaments with their mental traits are as follows: the sanguine, characterized by buoyant hope and strong self-confidence; the nervous, with rapid alternations of confidence and anxiety, prone to enthusiasm and to dejection; the phlegmatic, equally remote from the extremes of exaltation and despair, collected, temperate, and slow; and the bilious, inclined to take the gloomy view of events and to dwell on their darker side.

Most people can be classed under the one or the other of these, and the arrangement is not useless in self-culture, for it will furnish hints as to the manner of training required to correct unwholesome mental tendencies.

The temperament toward which they should all be modified is not included in the list. It is the *cheerful* temperament, that which is lighted by the rays of reasonable hope and a confidence in one's own powers grounded on a knowledge of their strength.

Cheerfulness, however, is a coy favorite, and is not to be had for the asking. It is a condition of mind which a man cannot think himself into, nor reason himself into, nor directly acquire by an effort of the will. No man can seat himself in his chair and say to himself,—"Go to! I will be merry!" It can in part be secured by a skillful disposition of the emotions at our command; but it is, in the main, the mental result of physical processes, and the profitable study of it must begin with these.

So very physical is it, that physiologists have undertaken to locate its exact seat in the human body. They place it in the great ganglia of the sympathetic nervous system, near the stomach and the heart, where also is located the seat of the sense of general miserableness that the French call *malaise.* No one feels happy in his head or in his foot; but we do speak of being light of heart, as well as heart-heavy and heart-broken. Those savage tribes who believe that the soul dwells in the pit of the stomach are not the worst physiologists.

The mental condition in certain diseases show how correct this is. Those which directly involve the stomach, the liver, the heart, and the intestinal canal are always associated with undue depression of spirits; while those which are confined to the lungs or the brain, though of the most fatal gravity, may be connected with undiminished cheerfulness. The *spes phthisica,* the hopefulness of the consumptive, is proverbial among physicians, but as deceptive to them as to others. A friend of mine, a medical man, who had fought this disease for three years, wrote me three days before his death, sketching a series of literary schemes which he had decided to undertake! Another malady of similar character is a variety of paralysis, always fatal, not uncommon among overworked business men of middle life. The patient will never acknowledge that he is ill or feels badly, and when so paralyzed that he cannot rise from his couch will insist that he is in splendid health and is merely lazy! How different from the dyspeptic, always magnifying his symptoms; from the hypochondriac with engorged liver; or from the sufferer from heart disease, with his long and inexplicable spells of low spirits!

The moral of these facts is evident. If we wish to have a cheerful disposition we must begin with attention to our physical functions. Even slight symptoms of dyspepsia, liver complaints, and disturbances of the digestive organs must receive appropriate treatment. In this country malarial poisoning is common, and as it spends its force on the spleen, it is always associated with low spirits. Hemorrhoids, which are usually connected with deficient action of the liver, and in women many diseases peculiar to their sex, act directly in inducing a condition of gloom and anxiety.

Of course, it is no part of my plan to suggest the proper treatment for these ails. But it does come within its purview to offer some hints to those who, without assignable physical cause, are subject to periodic depression of spirits, to what we familiarly call "an attack of the blues."

This is generally a reaction from mental overstrain or mental lethargy,—from the too intent pursuit of an object, or from having no object to pursue. A life without leisure and a life without labor are equally fatal to cheerfulness. The hurry and rush of business affairs, the atmosphere of excitement and unrest which surrounds them, are dangerous to a mind not extremely well poised. Not less so are the alternate phases of gloom and exaltation which attend religious revivals, prayer meetings, and the various manifestations of fanaticism. "That way madness lies," and our asylums show a heavy percentage of inmates who have lost their reason from religious excitement. The prolonged concentration of attention on one's heavenly interests is just as detrimental as on those of this world. Self-isolation is fatal; and anxiety for self-salvation is but one of its varieties.

While the multiplicity of rapid impressions leads to exhaustion and mental lassitude, variety and novelty are desirable. Change of diet is as salutary for the mind as for the body. One should have some agreeable occupation outside of his business, to which he can turn in his leisure moments and at the time when he quits active affairs. How many have I seen with enough to retire *on*, but with nothing to retire *to*! They are the unhappiest of mortals.

An occasional fit of depression can be broken by some simple measures. The hot bath is one of these. It is highly physiological, as its imperative summons of the nervous force to the periphery of the body breaks up the stagnation about the ganglionic centres. For the same reason the cold shower is excellent. No man leaves it in the same train of thought with which he entered it. Active exercise, society, games, and amusements will occur to all. Stimulants and narcotics are perilous palliatives. Better try Lord Lytton's advice, and resolutely attack a new language; or Ruskin's, to drive a restless horse or sail a cranky skiff, where the least inattention to what you have in hand means immediate danger to your life. You will have no time for the blues.

Self-preservation, I have said, is the prime condition of happiness. A long life, therefore, is the desire of all sane minds. Old age, that which all abhor, is the hope of all. It alone justifies a man to himself and before others. The sage is he whose life is a consistent whole, and who carries out in his age the plans which he laid in youth. They are not many; but even they deceive us by their number. On the ocean of existence, who counts the shipwrecked? We see the votive offerings of the saved displayed with ostentation, but who notes the number of the drowned? In the scenery of the drama of human life, the most conspicuous buildings are the hospitals and asylums, and into these sooner or later most of the actors disappear.

A learned French physician has maintained that the normal duration of human life is one hundred years; only a fifth of those born reach one half that age. Longevity is partly a birthright; it runs in families; but it is still more a question of occupation, mode of life, and personal hygiene. The Jews of Frankfurt average ten years more of life than the non-Jewish citizens, because they avoid unsanitary avocations and observe wiser rules of diet. I know a skillful physician who claims that he can lengthen the life of an individual a decade beyond the average of his ancestors by a judicious system of safeguards. Such an adviser is acquainted with the special dangers to which age is exposed. He knows, for instance, that at seventy-five exposure to cold is thirty-two times more dangerous than it is at thirty years of age.

The sorrows of age are usually the returns of the investments of youth, these proving of that sort which levy assessments instead of paying dividends. "A short life and a merry one," is the maxim of many a youngster. The hidden falsehood at the core of his philosophy is the belief that happiness belongs to youth alone. I have already referred to this dangerous fallacy. The bliss of youth, as portrayed by poets and romancers, did not belong to the youth I had, nor does it to the youths I know. The admiration of the early periods of life is one of a common class of illusions. There is greater charm in beauty half-concealed than wholly shown, in the dawn rather than in the day, in the promise of youth rather than in the maturity of manhood. Potentialities please more than actualities, because they excite our imagination and release us from the fetters of facts.

He who would work securely for his own welfare will not be led astray by the belief that any one period of life contains solely or in any large measure the enjoyments of life as a whole. He will, therefore, not eat to-day the bread of to-morrow. Rather he will consider the problem of life akin to a problem of Euclid, the *quod erat demonstrandum* of which is reached only in the last line. He will guard the fires of youth, that he may not in age have to sit by the cold ashes of exhausted pleasures.

Sad indeed is the fate of those men who live to outlive themselves. You find them in every community, and especially in those classes of society which offer the greatest opportunities for early liberty and enjoyment. They suffer from a kind of premature senility. They have fallen in the struggle, though they are not visibly wounded. To them, life has lost its zest and action its aim. Usually this is the result of the early exhaustion of irrational enjoyments; but it may proceed from some blow of disappointed ambition, from a violent shock to the emotions, from the vertigo of unlooked-for prosperity, or the discouragement of persistent adversity. The stroke has fallen, and no voice can awake them to action again.

The continuing satisfaction of an intense love of living,—that would be a fairly good definition of happiness, and not far from one which Fichte proposed.

Few at any age could say with Fontenelle at ninety-three,—"Had I my life to live again, I should change nothing."

What nobler compliment could be paid a man than this, which Vittoria Colonna wrote to Michael Angelo,—"You have disposed the labor of your whole life as one single great work of art."

No road is the right one to him who knows not whither he is going.

If you *will* stand in the rain, why pray the gods to keep you dry?

Many a defeat, claimed as a victory, passes for one.

Joys that are present are alone those that are real.

There is wisdom in the Spanish saying, "The water of your own village is better than the wine of Rome."

Think over this, that Walt Whitman wrote:—

> Will you seek afar off? You surely come back at last,
>
> In things best known to you finding the best, or as good as the best,
>
> In folks nearest to you finding the sweetest, strongest, lovingest,
>
> Happiness, knowledge, not in another place but in this place, not for another hour but this hour.

The two misfortunes of life are, that we are born young, and become old.

True, the mind of a child is a plot of virgin soil; but, like this, it is made up of strata of incalculable antiquity.

The moral lessons of our youth are like our old love letters,—carefully preserved, but never read.

Time wears out masks; the old show what they are.

The mellowest fruits of life should ripen in its autumn; but if the spring had not its seeding, and the summer its flowers, what harvest can we look for?

Many a man passes his youth in preparing misery for his age, and his age in repairing misconduct in his youth.

The old story says that the flowers you gather in Fairyland prove to be withered weeds on your return.

It is folly to be youthful unless you are young.

An old man who indulges in love-making had better derive his pleasure from his own sentiments, than from the hope that they will be reciprocated.

"Old men become frivolous," once said to me Weir Mitchell, poet, physician, philosophic observer of life. Yes, frivolous and sense-bound. Youth is earnest and spiritual, because it is sentient of creative force.

It is with health as with money; we wait till our stock is diminishing before we give it careful attention.

A Chinese proverb says, it is easy enough to die, but difficult to die at the right time. Many a man has lived to destroy his own well-earned reputation or fortune.

The danger of shipwreck is less in mid-ocean than near shore.

Hurry to reap ruins the harvest. To garner the grain we must bide from the sowing till the seed-time.

Pleasure is an expenditure of stored force. We must save up in order to have a good time. Nature is a merciless usurer, and demands heavy interest on her advances.

II. Our Physical Surroundings.

Palpably the nearest to us of all our physical surroundings is our clothing. Philosophers do not agree whether man originally adopted some covering for his body out of the desire of warmth, the sense of modesty, or the love of decoration. Enough that at present all these motives are operative, and all are to be respected.

The first purpose of clothing is to preserve the health by keeping out the cold. There is more in this than mere comfort. Warm clothing economizes nervous energy, which otherwise has to be expended on the extremities of the nerves to maintain the capillaries in activity. A man when comfortably warm can think more clearly than when he feels chilly. Mind and body are alike benumbed by extreme cold. Exposure to even a moderately low temperature is dangerous to the aged and the frail. Those who have studied the meteorology of health have established the maxim,—"Waves of cold are waves of death."

In his clothing the sensible man will conform to the customs and station of society in which he moves. He will leave to his tailor the cut of his coat. It is a sign of greater weakness to affect a fashion of one's own than to follow that of others. He will not be without a dress suit in civilized lands, and will not wear top boots in drawing rooms, as did in London a semi-celebrated American poet.

A century or two ago the dress of men was far more costly and significant. That they have now adopted a simple and uniform style shows that higher interests are occupying their minds. The first sign that women are approaching the same level will be their enfranchisement from the slavery of dress and fashion, to which so many of them devote the best part of their lives. To woman, clothing will always be more a question of art than utility. But most of the modes which she now follows are caricatures of art. For them, however, she will sacrifice not only good taste but good morals. Vanity in dress, not the deception of men, leads the majority of fallen women to their life. They feel more degraded by an unbecoming costume than by a tarnished reputation.

A man changes his character with his garments. Dirty clothes excuse dirty actions. I heard of a carpenter who was at a fire where he could easily have carried off articles; but he explained that he had on his best clothes, and that prevented him. The reason why sermons have so little effect is that we lay aside our Sunday suits on Monday morning. This is the value of uniform. Dress a hundred men alike, and they will think alike. The character is subdued to what 'tis clothed in. Outward, develops inward conformity. The world recognizes this, and accepts the clothing as the index of the mind. A well-dressed man is supposed to be a gentleman, and an officer with sword and epaulettes is regarded as a tactician and a hero. Would you change the current of your thoughts, change your raiment, and you will at once feel the effect. Would you assuage your grief, lay aside your mourning.

Next to our clothing, our immediate surroundings are the room and its furniture. A third of our lives is passed in our sleeping apartment, and most of the remainder in sitting-room, library, or office. It is well worth while, therefore, to give it attention. How much pleasure it can be made to render! The genial Xavier de Maistre consumed a month in making his celebrated *Voyage autour de ma Chambre*, and then regretted his time was so short. What harmonies of light and color, shade and perspective, even the humblest adornment of a room is capable of yielding! How each article of furniture comes to take its place in our lives and memories! The clock, the desk, the lounge, these are what make up the sense of Home. Even the noble sentiment of patriotism is founded upon them. To defend our hearth is its intimate purpose, and love of our easy-chair is a large share of our love of country. To all women and many men the most constant happiness of life is centred in the room and its furniture. Here is the temple of the Goddess of the Household, and her name should be Lætitia.

How much, therefore, depends on the selection of our living rooms! They should be light, bright, dry, airy, well-ventilated, equably warmed, appropriately furnished, free from bad odors, far from brutal noises, screened from impertinent curiosity. All these requirements ought to be easily obtained and at no great cost. But so little does modern architecture consider the true comfort and the real happiness of house-dwellers that it is rare that one can find all combined.

If he can, therefore, the wise man will prefer to build his own house. Some will question this. Somewhere in his works—they are too voluminous for me to look up the reference—Rousseau argues that a philosopher will not desire a house of his own, but will prefer to live in one that is rented. He will thus consult his independence, be free to come and go, not engage his affections on inanimate objects, find his fatherland wherever he may be, and the like.

For myself, I incline rather to the opinion of Abraham Cowley, less of a philosopher than Rousseau but more in sympathy with the general sentiments of mankind. I agree with him that "the pleasantest work of human industry is the improvement of something which we may call our own." There is something in itself delightful in the mere sense of ownership of a part of the surface of the earth. It was not mere greed in Cosmo de Medici, who, when asked why he preferred his villa in the Apennines to his palace in Florence, replied,—"Because there, every foot of land I see is my own." No prospect is quite so pleasing as that of our own acres, and those governments are strongest which base their institutions on the personal tenure of land.

The old proverb prescribes the chief duties of a man to be to build a house and beget a child. The character of his child he can but slightly control; the plan of his house is in his own hands, and his health and happiness are deeply involved in it. "He that builds a fair house on an ill site," observes Bacon, "committeth himself to prison;" and I may add, he that builds an ill house on any site, sends himself and family to a hospital. One half of the deaths in England are from preventable causes, and one-half of these are causes connected with defective house building. The most perfect buildings are the gaols. Both in England and America the best care is taken of the worst men. The chances of life for the convict who is in prison is seven times better than when he is at liberty. If health is the highest good, we had better all apply to be sent to gaol.

The principal foes to fight are dampness, darkness, chilliness, draughtiness, insufficient ventilation, sewer-gas or other poisonous effluvia, contaminated or scanty water supply, and unhealthful situation. Architects know little about these matters. Decorative effects rather than sanitary perfection are what occupy their attention. Every house-builder should be his own architect to the extent of clearly knowing what he wants, and seeing that it is looked after in the plans.

A beautiful feature of American life is the ease with which every one can acquire his own home. Rapid transit facilitates this even for those who dwell in great cities.

The possession of his own house is within the reasonable ambition of every man, and should ever form a part of it. What if it must be a small house? He can say with Socrates—"Lucky me, if I have friends enough to fill it!"

"Cosiness!" how much that word implies! What pictures of intimate delights it brings before the mind! But who can imagine it in great, straggling mansions, or in "palace chambers far apart"? In the vast and gloomy palace of the Escorial, the only rooms I saw which would not induce an attack of melancholia to live in were a suite not larger than those in an ordinary American house, in which the royal family sought escape from the pressure of their own magnificence in their occasional visits to this famous pile. Happiness dwells not in spacious halls and stately apartments, and he who seeks it will not envy their possessors.

Has a house ever been built with an eye solely to the highest happiness of its inmates? to their health, sometimes; to their comfort, occasionally; to the parade of their riches, constantly; but to their happiness? I doubt. Conveniences, sanitary arrangements, agreeable vistas, balconies, porches, fireplaces, these would not be omitted, but would be merely the beginning of the plan. How to conciliate isolation with social relations, how to promote harmony between those serving and those served, how to provide that the employments of one do not jar with those of others, these would be some of the questions to consider. How many family troubles could be avoided by a properly built house! Faulty architecture is more frequently the ruin of family felicity than is heterodox doctrine.

The Greeks called man the "earth-born," and the love of his native place is ever one of the most responsive of his heartstrings. Some say it is lacking in Americans, because they are so restless, but this is an error. The poor boy who wanders away from his native village to make his fortune does not forget the scenes of his childhood, and should his dreams be realized, returns to the old familiar places to leave at least some token of his affection. More than half the public libraries in New England towns have been given wholly or in large part by those who were to the manor born, but who had found fortune under strange skies.

The scenery of our dreams is generally that with which we were first familiar, and the dying old man babbles of the green fields of his boyhood. We may admire grand views from foreign belvederes, but those which we first saw remain unsurpassed. I crossed the ocean with an intelligent woman returning from the Rhine and the Alps; but her longing was for the vast, treeless prairies of Illinois, her girlish home, where sky meets earth all round the horizon, and the soul feels no confinement of mountains or forests.

Love of place rather than love of persons leads to the unhappy condition of homesickness. As "nostalgia," it becomes an actual disease of body and mind, and men will die of it, unless allowed to return to their native land. Haunting, imperious thirst of the soul for the scenes of its early pleasures! Heaven cannot be imagined without them.

The thoughtful writer, Herder, who was the first to cultivate history as the seed-field of philosophy, was of opinion that it is less the earth on which we tread, than the air we breathe, which gives the peculiar charm to the scenes of childhood; meaning that it is the climate, and the sequence of the seasons which leave the chief impress on the budding observation of our surroundings. The eternal summer of the tropics becomes monotonous to the native of temperate latitudes, and the Eskimo or the Laplander in the more genial climes pines for the short, hot summer and bitter winter to which he has been accustomed. The desire, therefore, for more favorable climates, except for purposes of health, is an illusion. The "summer isles of Eden" would fatigue with their monotony and enervate by their excellence. The enjoyment of life is independent of the thermometer, if we determine it shall be. Sunshine within more than compensates for its absence without.

By climate we usually mean the weather, and this unquestionably exerts a powerful influence on human happiness. That of most portions of the United States keeps the character which William Penn gave it two hundred years ago—"constant in nothing but inconstancy." Many a project of pleasure does it mar, and many a discomfort does it create! but in its very changeableness there is something attractive, as always lurks in the unexpected. If we travel the same road every day in the year, on no two are sky and landscape the same. Daily, new scenes are offered to our sight, each with its peculiar charm, if we take the trouble to look for it. Almost can one reason himself into an equality with that unapproachable philosopher, the Shepherd of Salisbury Plain, who, when asked what the weather would be on the morrow, replied that it would be just what he preferred; and on further inquiry as to what this might be, triumphantly answered, "Whatever the Lord sends."

On some temperaments, a low barometer produces a peculiarly depressing effect. The advice often given them is to make renewed exertion at their customary employments, and combat the disinclination with the Will. My advice would be more agreeable; they should lay aside the customary routine, if possible, and seek in change, recreation, and amusements the cheerfulness which their ordinary employment refuses them. Do not spur the jaded horse, but rather offer repose and variety of motion.

The pressure of the atmosphere as indicated by the barometer has a great deal to do directly with health and spirits, and therefore with happiness. Those with a tendency to heart disease should seek a residence at the sea level, while many who have weak lungs will improve where the air is rarefied by a high altitude. What the Swiss call *le mal des montagnes* is a general sense of discomfort which some feel a few thousand feet above the sea, and which even prolonged residence does not entirely banish. An asthmatic can have no pleasure in life unless he finds the climate where he can breathe with comfort.

Worst of all for personal happiness is a malarial climate, and, unfortunately, they are very common in this country. The miasmatic poison is peculiarly depressing to the mind, and is always associated with debility and despondency. Malarial regions cannot be left uninhabited, but those whose evil fortune it is to be condemned to dwell in them have a heavy additional burden laid upon them in life.

We are all more or less like those lower animals whose colors change with their surroundings.

Seek the open air; the fruits which grow outdoors are alone those which ripen in season.

He who loves his country more than he does his kind, loves himself more than either.

To die for our country is truly noble, when our country is the world and our fellow-citizens all mankind.

Love of country is sometimes a fine phrase for love of comfort.

Woman, like the Emperor Tiberius, is smothered with clothes.

Woman is philocosmic because she is philanthropic.

Fine clothes are the stilts to individuality.

A new suit is a new sensation.

We do not wholly leave our bed-room all day long.

Make the places you must occupy as pleasure-giving as possible.

Frugality is never better displayed than in furnishing.

Outdoors, let Action rule in the ascendant; indoors, Repose.

Houses used to be built to protect from foes without; the need now is more protection for friends within.

III. Luck and its Laws.

When the wisest of the seven wise men of Greece was asked to name some happy person, he cited several, all of whom were among the dead. "And do you know none living who is happy?" queried his royal host, who had expected his own name to be mentioned among the fortunate few. "Call no man happy," replied the sage, "until he is dead." He forgot not that in the temples of his native land, Tyche, Goddess of Chance, was represented holding in one hand a rudder, for it is she who guides the affairs of men; but in the other hand a sphere, to warn of the instability of her favors. Like the King of Lydia, most of her modern votaries remember her former but forget her latter attribute.

Science preaches that the progress of thought has been from a time when Caprice and Chance were deemed everything in nature and Law was nothing, to the present day, when Law is known to be everything and Caprice and Chance are nothing.

Science may preach till it is hoarse, but there is something in the human mind ever insisting that the ancient Goddess, or some other inscrutable fatality, coerces the history of the individual; and that, from his birth, luck, good or bad, merriment or melancholy, marks him for her own. Rarely have I asked a man of large experience who denied the mighty influence of the unforeseen and unforeseeable in practical affairs. Some of the most extensive enterprises are based on the recognition of this truth, and it is mathematically demonstrable; for mathematicians are prepared to show that disorder itself is orderly, and that the vagaries of chance are bound by laws, and pinned in a straight jacket of formulas.

But what their apparatus of signs and symbols does not show, where it completely breaks down, is precisely the only point of human interest in the whole matter,—in its application to the individual life and fortunes. Averages and general laws they give us; but it is also a mathematical law that the average is never applicable to the individual. What is true of the whole series is never true of any one member of the series. No man who insured his life ever died at the precise minute which, according to the actuary's tables, terminated his calculable expectation of life.

Let us see what, from this point of view, these computations about luck or chance teach.

In mathematics they are included in the Calculus of Probabilities, the discovery of which is attributed to Pascal. A gambling nobleman asked him what are the chances of turning a red or black card in cutting the pack a given number of times. As all the cards are either red or black, Pascal replied that it would be expressed by the formula x/2. In ordinary language, this means that when two events are equally probable, they will occur equally in the long run; and in practical affairs, when we neither know nor suspect things are unequal, we must assume them to be equal.

On these simple principles all calculations of chances, to be worth anything, must be based. But they are not so simple as they sound. Pascal's formula, like all formulas of the higher mathematics, expresses an abstract truth only, and one that can never be realized in fact. The longer the run, the more certain will it be that the two events never will occur equally; and the more frequent will be long series of the recurrence of one or the other.

Turning aside from abstruse calculations, which can be readily found elsewhere by those who would like to see them, let us inquire as to the practical results of this Logic of Chance when applied to the fortunes of the individual.

These observed and calculated results establish the following interesting rule:—In matters of pure luck, about two-thirds of any given number of persons will come out substantially even, in any large number of trials; of the remaining third, about one-half will be noticeably lucky, and the remaining one-half noticeably unlucky. Thus, of six who venture, four will have no special fortune, good or bad; one will be quite "in vein"; one quite "out of vein."

Suppose the players are thirty-six, and we select the lucky six, and pit them against each other, as in "progressive" games; the same law will hold good, one coming out noticeably better, one noticeably worse than the rest; and so on indefinitely, the number of the extremes diminishing at the rate of six to one at each new trial.

This is the Law of Luck; but it is obvious that it leaves luck, good and bad, a real fact; and among a million men, or in a great city like New York or London, we must find extraordinary examples of "sequences," both of the favors and the frowns of fortune; not in gambling only, but in those thousands of accidental events which make up the welfare or misery of personal experience.

All the moralists I have read on the subject seem to blink and stagger at this obvious and necessary conclusion,—that the history of many individuals is and must be enormously controlled, in spite of any efforts of their own, by pure luck. In cutting the cards twenty times in succession, about twenty people in a million will cut red every time and another twenty will cut black every time; and so it will be with all other matters of pure chance in life. There is no use in trying to dodge this certain result of a sum in simple division. We must count it in, in all plans and calculations for success and happiness in our individual life.

The important question is, what value must we assign to it?

Here is where men make several frequent and disastrous errors.

The most common is an error in arithmetic which the little I have above said on the calculus of chance should be enough to correct. It is putting faith in their good luck, or falling into discouragement from their bad luck. Each is equally silly. A sequence of any kind of luck does not offer the slightest presumption that it will continue. The chances remain precisely as at the beginning, and are about six to one against the continuance of either extreme in the same individual. In matters of pure chance no sustained coincidence in either direction adds the least probability to its continuance. This is what is so difficult for men to believe; and so it comes about that faith in good luck is the source of most bad luck. A "run of good luck" has wrecked the lives of more men than has the repetition of disasters.

The reason for this is easily shown. The general rule in life is that a man's prosperity is conditioned closely by the amount and kind of his knowledge, and his skill in the use of it. But the man who "trusts to luck" distinctly renounces the advantages of knowledge, and builds his hopes on his acknowledged impotence to influence the results. He abandons himself to the current of events, and makes no effort to look forward and see whether it will suck him into a whirlpool, or land him on some sunny shore. Scarcely any state of mind could be fraught with greater peril to his future.

We have the sayings, "dumb luck" and "a fool for luck;" and the Italians their proverb that one must have a little of the fool in him, *un poco di matto*, to be lucky. Most men are fools, so it is inherently probable that the lucky man will belong to the majority; but beyond that, *his* folly is conspicuous who bases his hopes of fortune rather on luck than on labor and forethought. The immorality of gambling and its ruinous influence on the happiness of life lie in the fact that it disclaims as useless every precept which prudence, skill, and knowledge lay down as essential to individual success.

It is mathematically certain that some people will have an astonishing succession of fortunate experiences which they have nowise aided in bringing about, ripe plums dropping into their mouths from invisible trees. They are popularly called "lucky fellows." But the ancient Greeks, with that wonderful acumen in practical affairs which was their own, considered them peculiarly dangerous associates, to be avoided as partners in regular business, scarcely safe to associate with as companions. When Polycrates, King of Samos, was crowned with such repeated successes that it seemed as if the very gods might envy him, his friend, the King of Egypt, advised him to throw his most precious jewel, a wonderfully carved signet-ring, into the sea; and when this was brought back the next day by a fisherman, who had found it in the belly of a fish that had swallowed it, the King of Egypt withdrew his fleet and severed his treaty; for he knew some dreadful disaster awaited such unheard-of fortune; and it soon came when Polycrates fell into the hands of his enemy, and was crucified alive on the Asian strand.

The story is probably a fable; but its moral is an eternal truth. The hour of prosperity is ever dangerous; but when the prosperity has come without labor or effort or forethought, it is nearly always fatal. Unexpected success enervates the will and fosters illusions of the mind. The ancients represented the goddess Fortuna as proffering a cup of intoxicating wine to her favorites. Either they recognize their success as the result of pure chance, and persuade themselves that they are fortune's favorite children, and can safely hazard any risks; or their vanity leads them to attribute what was the result of chance to their own miraculous sagacity, and they thus magnify to a dangerous degree their own capacities. Either conclusion leads them surely on the downward road to ruin.

Nowhere is this mental debility which seizes the believers in luck more absurdly shown than in the return to primeval superstition which it brings with it. The gambler, in his faith in caprice and chance, sinks to the level of the primitive savage, and accepts the superstitions of that level with equal readiness. The most cultivated habitué of Monte Carlo has his fetishes; he watches for signs and omens; he is as much the slave of auspicious or inauspicious auguries as an Australian cannibal. Pitiable retrogression of the human intellect! What absurdity will he not commit to "break the run of the luck" when it is against him! He will turn his chair thrice around; he will avoid playing if a red-whiskered man opposite him stakes; he will go to his hotel and change his coat. He knows that every principle of right reason and sound logic teaches that events cannot be modified by actions in no way relating to them, but he quietly renounces reason and logic as his guides!

Surely no man who is engaged in the intelligent pursuit of happiness will put himself in that position! I do not forget the pleasure of the game. That will be considered on a later page. But there is no need to argue that a pleasure which leads to the habitual disregard of reason as a monitor cannot be trusted as a permanent contributor to happiness.

One important practical point remains to be noted. Neither in the gambling room, nor outside, is there half so much mere luck in affairs as most people imagine. The cards are stacked, the dice are loaded, the balls are weighted. Only the gulls believe the game is fair. Shrewd men in business transactions like to conceal their hands, and persuade their clients and associates that much is the result of accident which they themselves have brought about. The plan has many advantages, and plays successfully on the most responsive chords of human weakness. It is said that the late Baron Rothschild of London declined to embark in an enterprise unless its promoters were known as lucky men. Do not imagine that he was governed by any foolish superstition. He knew, perhaps better than any one, what is the real significance of constant luck in the stock market; and would have been the last to have accepted it in the sense of the guileless gambler.

Much that in the lives of others we are apt to attribute to luck turns out on closer examination to be the natural though infrequent result of certain cultivated qualities. I have heard of several persons who have had handsome legacies left them by strangers in unexpected acknowledgment of kindness shown. Uniform courtesy is almost sure to be followed sooner or later by some such reward. People who are what we call "quick-witted," whose judgment is cool and action prompt, are apt to be lucky even in misfortune. William of Normandy, landing for the conquest of England, tripped and fell on the sand. It was an evil presage, and his soldiers shrank back in terror. But William, seizing a handful of the soil, cried—"Thus I grasp this earth, and, by the splendor of God, I shall keep it." With this he turned the gloomy portent into one the most auspicious. Moderate luck with good sense will repair any blunder, while folly will spoil the best of chances. "Fortune favors the bold," simply because they have the courage to act; but she rarely favors them when they act without knowledge and prudence. When Shakespeare in the familiar passage says, "There is a tide in the affairs of men, which taken at the flood leads on to fortune," he assumes that the fortunate man knows when flood-tide arrives.

As we are thus often deceived in the lives of others, so we are almost as frequently the dupes of our own experience. It is not easy to decide, concerning our successes and failures, which are owing to luck and which to ourselves. Confucius advises those who fail to follow the example of the archer when he misses the target, and examine first the instruments employed, and then themselves, as the cause of failure is likely to be in one or the other. Some minds are more exhilarated by gains than they are depressed by losses; others deplore losses more keenly than they enjoy successes; few estimate both at a just relative value.

Even the very unlucky should feel some cheerfulness when he reflects how in modern times we have learned to conciliate the Fates, and compel even the most adverse destiny to drop the ugliest of its masks. This we accomplish through the various forms of *insurance*, all of them based on the study of the very caprices of Fortune herself. Marvelous example of mind setting at nought the threats of brute nature! The very disasters before which our ancestors bowed most hopeless and most helpless, are those whose attacks we dread the least. Hail and lightning, storms on the ocean and fire in populous cities, we read about with small concern providing our property is well insured. By the same process we can protect our children from poverty and our own old age from want. Beneficent discovery, which in its varied forms has added incalculably to the happiness of man by freeing him from the terrors of the unknown, and providing him with a shield behind which he can afford to smile at the gloomiest frowns of Fate!

Subtler than any beast of the field is man, and filled with Promethean courage to rob the gods themselves! But behind the impenetrable veil, through which he sees not even darkly, are powers who smile in derision at his attempts to free himself from their eternal mastery. No logic can explain and no calculus compute the workings of their mysterious ways. Against the elemental wrath of fire and water man can guard himself; but against the results of the most thoughtless of his words or the slightest of his actions he has no protection, for he has not and cannot form the least idea of their consequences. Here Destiny rules undisputed and supreme.

Such reflections led the great Goethe in his old age to dwell more and more on the illimitable influence of trifling events, *bedeutende Kleinigkeiten*. Dull critics have misunderstood and some of the dullest have even made merry about his insistence on this pivotal truth in the history of every individual and in that of the world. The fate of nations has ever been decided by the most trivial occurrences. Cæsar, going to the Senate, refused to read a letter which was handed him, saying, "Business for to-morrow." Had he opened it, the greatest empire that ever was would have had a different story to transmit to a different posterity. One summer morning the pretty Arleta, daughter of a Norman butcher, tripped down to the brook to wash her mother's soiled linen. Had she waited a few minutes later, Robert the Devil would have already passed, and neither their son, the bastard William of Normandy, nor his thousands of knights would have set their iron heels on English soil. Louis XVI stops at St. Ménéhould to eat a pig's foot, and the great and famous line of the Bourbons of France is extinguished by that single dish.

These are celebrated examples. But the thoughtful man will recognize in his own life and in the lives of those around him how they have been altered, directed, completely transformed by such slightest of incidents. His decision to pursue this or that avocation, that as to where he should settle, the first meeting with her who is his wife, the conversation which led to such or such an investment of the first importance, these, the most momentous actions of his life, turned on such casual and insignificant incidents that it makes him shiver to think of it! In such moments he is ready to exclaim,

"We do confess ourselves the slaves of chance

And flies of every wind that blows."

The prime motors of the thought of the world have not been the ponderous tomes of schoolmen nor the decrees of councils and universities. What, asks a philosophical historian, were the two most important events in the intellectual history of England during the seventeenth century? The Paradise Lost? The King James' Version? No. One was the commitment of a strolling tinker to Bedford Jail; the other the decision of a distempered youth to make himself a coat of leather and go to live in a hollow tree. The one gave us the "Pilgrim's Progress;" the other the immortal doctrine that faith, the true faith, "finds center everywhere," and cares not to fix itself in form.

"Slaves of Chance!" Of Chance? Have I the right word? Is it Chance which through millions of years has steadily guided the increasing purpose which runs through all nature, which has multiplied the organs of animals and widened the minds of men with the progress of the suns; which has disabled the armies of kings by the weaponless words of a peasant; which has confounded wisdom by folly and foiled strength by weakness; never anywhere losing sight of the goal, unseen of men but surely divined, toward which tends the Motion of the World?

Chance? No. But by what other name shall I name it? Shall I take refuge in the jargon of the pulpit and call these "special providences?" Helpless evasion of the question! Impotent effort to distinguish between the special and the general designs of the Designer, obscuring the one central point to be kept in sight, that the special is the general and the general the special.

But why seek a name? A name becomes a fetish as much as a stock or a stone, and men bow down to it and worship it with as much abasement of their better natures. Enough, if in the fates of mighty nations and in each lightest act of the individual life we recognize the same Directing Force, invisible but nowise unintelligible, rather speaking with sun-clear words to our enlightened reason of conscious purpose and definite intention, to which the iron laws of Nature and the wild vagaries of Chance are ductile instruments and obedient servants.

This is the ultimate expression of abstract science and of that solid philosophy which is built on the inductive study of both nature and man.

Its lesson to the individual is, that he is neither the helpless creature of necessity nor the slave of chance; that he is master of his immediate action, but of its consequences he is not master; that there are unseen forces at work arranging the incidents and accidents of his life, and these forces he can in no wise control; but if he is alert and diligent they cannot entangle his own individuality in the mesh of events, he can rise superior to them, can be *himself*, and win happiness to some degree in any surroundings; and he may go forward in the sublime and certain confidence that his existence is an essential part of an eternal plan, which asks neither faith nor authority for its recognition, for it is the logical condition of the very reason by which he knows that he is Himself and not another.

The calculus of probabilities has already destroyed the gods; if it could rule out the unexpected, it would promote man to their seats; but the fleshless face of old Time wears a perpetual though silent grin.

Fortune-tellers are put in jail because they deceive; they should be hanged, did they tell the truth. How dull were life, could it be read ahead! Only a weak nature, such as his, would say with Hartley Coleridge, "Happiness is the exclusion of all *hap*, that is, chance." More virile are the words of Charles James Fox, inveterate gambler that he was, "The next best thing to winning is to lose." The uncertainty of the future is the only stimulus to exertion, and its obscurity is the source of our chief delights.

Always expect a change of luck. Then, if it is from good to bad, you will be prepared for it; and if from bad to good, you will have enjoyed the pleasure of expecting it, as well as its arrival.

"Give your son luck and throw him in the sea," says a Spanish proverb.

There are men who succeed thro*ugh their misfortunes rather than their good fortunes.*

People regard bad luck as *a kin*d of injustice. They secretly say with Louis XIV, when his armies were defeated in Flanders, "Has God forgotten all I have done for Him?"

The ancients reckoned a man's luck, good or bad, among the gifts with which he is endowed by nature.

In very strong characters there is something which eludes analysis and defies definition, the very goad of destiny, driving them on their allotted paths with unrelenting *and i*nevitable impulse. This is what the ancient Greeks, and among the moderns especially Goethe, recognized as the "demonic force." It endows a life with dramatic unity and historic completeness.

Fate lies in fetters, so *she* no longer rules the stage.

The folly of some men *turns* out better than the foresight of others.

With Courage and Civility *as allies* you can often take captive Good-luck.

He who has *well cons*idered all the chances is prepared for the worst.

Because one cannot see ahead clearly, should he put out his eyes?

The captain who prefers trusting to luck to taking an observation is not the man to sail with.

Bacon advises to use such as have been lucky because of the confidence they breed in others and the effort they will make "to maintain their presc*ription*."

The first principle of success in the game of life is to be willing to lose. The player who *will* not sacrifice his pawns will soon have his king in check.

Keep your wits about you. In the immediate exigencies of life a full pocketbook is more useful than a fine bank balance.

Do you ever ask yourself why you expect good fortune to come without effort and bad fortune to stay away without precautions?

PART III.

How far our Happiness depends on Ourselves.

I. Our Occupations, those of Necessity and those of Choice.

In one of his novels, Emile Zola describes a conversation between the workwomen of a Parisian laundry. The subject was, what each would do if she had ten thousand francs a year. They were all of one mind. They would do just nothing at all!

This washerwoman's ideal of happiness has also commended itself to various philosophic minds. "I have often said," writes Pascal, "that all misfortunes befall men because they do not know enough to stay quietly in their own rooms." What puzzled him was that men will make the most toilsome efforts to secure a period of repose; and as soon as they obtain it, they weary of it and demand action. He might have learned from this the fallacy of his own definition.

The genial Herder taught that simplicity and repose are the two valves of the shell that secretes the pearl of human felicity; but he neglected to add that it must be the simplicity of aims combined with a multiplicity of means; and repose enjoyed merely as a preparation for renewed activity.

The true doctrine is that Labor, systematic, effective, congenial Labor, is not only a necessity, it is the source of the highest enjoyment to men. The ancients were right when they said the gods sell all pleasures at the price of toil. "Function in healthful action" is the definition which the modern physiologist gives of the feeling of pleasure; and he but translates into prose the poetic expression of the old Greek. The elements of true happiness must be sought in activity, not in repose; and it is high time that the world and the wiseacres found it out, and ceased singing peans to idleness and cursing the necessity of work.

Most men and a great many women have to work for their living. They usually accept the necessity with discontent and with envy of those who are idle or are in other pursuits. The farmer thinks he would have done better to have gone to the city. The lawyer regrets that he did not study medicine. As in Dr. Johnson's story:—

"Surely," said Rasselas, "the wise men to whom we listen with reverence chose that mode of life for themselves which they thought most likely to make them happy."

"Very few," replied the poet, "live by choice. Every man is placed in his present condition by causes which acted without his foresight, and with which he did not always co-operate."

In this country most men select for themselves the occupation which they pursue for a livelihood; but I doubt whether the freedom in their choice makes them more contented with it. The root of their discontent lies deeper than is suggested in Dr. Johnson's philosophic tale, and its removal, so indispensable to personal happiness, must be sought for elsewhere than in still wider license of choosing.

So far as either happiness or success is concerned it makes no difference, in nine cases out of ten, what business or profession a young man adopts, so that it is suitable to his education and social position. The rare exceptions are where there is some strong natural bent or aptitude; and even then the pursuit of it is more likely to bring enjoyment than money. Men are about equally fitted by nature for all the ordinary avocations of life, and the choice of a business is less important than is generally believed.

That is not where the secret of success and happiness lies. It lies in learning to practice one's trade or profession as an art, to like it for its own sake, to derive a considerable portion of our pleasure from its pursuit, to have, as the French say, our heart in it, *Avoir le cœur au métier*. But how is this possible, one will ask, with the drudgery of the counting house, or the mill, or the harvest field, or the Court of Quarter Sessions? It is possible with any avocation, if one will take the trouble to think about it as one of the manifold branches of human industry, to study its relations to other branches and to the lives and fates of human beings, to try to improve it, and to learn its attractions for those who do like it, and endeavor to enter into their feelings. Every occupation has some such attractions and some such possibilities. Those who are willing to see and seize them are those who derive both solid enjoyment and substantial rewards from their work.

Another secret lies in the cultivation of a sort of analogy or harmony between our mental disposition and the occurrences and surroundings in which our obligatory labor places us. This is quite within our own power to effect by the voluntary control of our thoughts. Why busy our imaginations and disturb our minds with dreaming of the pleasures of foreign travel when we know we have to stay at home and work ten hours a day? Far better occupy ourselves with the interests around us and the easily attainable pleasures within our reach. Have no fear that this course is narrowing or lowering. There are no nobler games than those which can be played on any village lawn, and the hyssop on your garden wall, could you read it, would teach you the laws of all organic nature.

The considerations which should have weight in the choice of avocation are less those of capacity or inclination, since these differ little and can readily be cultivated, than those referred to on an earlier page which relate to health, bodily and mental. It is not necessary to be very clever to succeed in business; only a little more clever than those around you. But it is necessary to have your health; for in the struggle for bread, the weak are thrust to the wall without remorse. No one who chooses wisely will select a business which will aggravate an hereditary or acquired malady. It is more satisfactory to be honor-man of a lower class, than come in at the tail-end of a higher one.

There are also certain mental disqualifications which apply especially to the professions. William Hazlitt objected to all professions which depend on reputation, because this is "as often got without merit as lost without deserving;" but this is less the case now than it was formerly. The point is rather a mental unfitness for the work required, a state of things which may exist with plenty of ability. The politician with an instinctive shrinking from publicity, the lawyer who has an aversion to argument, the physician who is unable to show sympathy and interest where he feels none, may succeed in his profession, but he will scarcely enjoy it.

Intense application to an occupation is a common cause of distaste for it and unhappiness in it. Such concentration is nearly always needless, and is often fruitless. The most brilliant fortunes have not been the products of hard work, but of shrewd planning. The sweetness of the chimes does not depend on the violence of the ringing, but on the skill of the bellman. I had a friend who was brought up a broker, but remained a philosopher. He used to say that energy in business is the most common cause of failures. He referred, of course, to that exclusive and persistent zeal which is pretty sure to end by enfeebling the body and exhausting the mind.

Dissatisfaction with one's lot sometimes arises from over conscientiousness, — a rare disease, I confess, in business circles, but I have met a few cases of it. "Always try to do your best," is one of several hundred copy-book maxims which hypocrisy pretends are necessary to success, but which common sense and practical life quietly ignore. Very much less than your best will often answer the purpose, and the rope that reaches is long enough. I have witnessed considerable distress, especially among young men, because their books of account were not so immaculate, or their press-articles so studied, as they might have been by greater toil; yet they were good enough,—and good enough is good.

At the best, making one's living is often a sad affair. Business life is like a dinner at a crowded third-rate hotel, —one's clothing is so torn in the struggle for place, and there is so much dirt to eat before the dessert is served, that either the appetite turns to nausea, or its satisfaction is followed by indigestion. Hence so many able men prefer permanent positions on small salaries to embarking in affairs on their own account. Many a lawyer will give up a large practice to become a judge on one-third of the income. Politics in the United States is, as a business, notoriously unsafe, but the attraction of fixed salaries overcrowds it with aspirants. The dream of the Socialists is for all citizens to be salaried. Individual effort, however, alone insures general progress; not to dispense with it, but to favor its pleasurable development, is the real social problem.

The true aim of Occupations of Necessity is to provide us time, not for repose and inaction, as most moralists teach, but for Occupations of Choice. We call these our recreations, amusements, pastimes, favorite studies, hobbies, fads, if you please. In these lie the mainsprings of our felicity; and their character reveals pretty clearly the measure of our capacity for happiness, and the degree of our mastery of its theory. If we pass our leisure in cultivating delusions and pursuing inanities, our enjoyment is that of the insane and the idiotic, and arises not from the health, but from the disease or debility, of our minds. Yet how many men, skillful in securing the means of pleasure, are witless in the use of it!

"Those are the best recreations," says old Thomas Fuller, "which, besides refreshing, enable men to some other good ends." His words, though they sound well, are only half-wise. To enjoy to the utmost any favorite pastime or study, it should be pursued for itself alone, and with no ulterior purpose or hope in view. "'Twere to cramp its use, to hook it to some useful end." Pleasure is nobler than profit, enjoyment is higher than utility, whatever political economists or pulpit orators say to the contrary. I know some men who always explain their relaxations as a part of their serious lives; and others who, if detected in an act of benevolence, hasten to show that it was prompted by their self-interest; of the two, I admire the latter more.

Success is another name for Perseverance. When Newton was asked how he reached his great discovery, he replied, "By making it incessantly the subject of my thoughts."

Happiness follows success, provided the latter is rightly achieved and received.

A contented spirit is merely one which pleases itself with little effort. Contentment differs from Happiness, as repose from recreation.

For most, it will be easier to learn to like what they have to do, than to find the chance of doing what they like.

To teach what they do not know, and to live by a trade that they do not understand, are feats that many are surprised that they cannot perform.

All paths seem rough to the bare feet of those who are used to wearing shoes.

Would you have pleasant yesterdays and welcome to-morrows, let to-day be busy and confident.

You may pound away with the hammer, but if you are not driving a nail, you will break instead of building.

Most divers bring up mud; but few, pearls.

The honey which we gather ourselves tastes the sweetest.

The measure of value of work is the amount of play it provides for; the measure of value of play is the amount of work there is in it.

Play-time should be perfecting-time; the use of leisure hours is to get rid of the lees of life.

Before all days are made holidays, all men should become heroes.

II. Money-making, its Laws and its Limits.

There are some prayers which belong to the universal Religion of Humanity, and none more so than this, which is found in the oldest prayer-book of the Aryan race, the Rig Veda,—"O Lord, prosper us in the getting and the keeping!" "To make money" is certainly the "soul's sincere desire" of most citizens of the world at the present day, and nowhere is it more fervently uttered than in this country.

This is no discredit. So far as we can trace the history of man from the Old Stone Age upward, the one efficient motive to his progress has been the acquisition and preservation of property. This has been the immediate aim of all his arts and institutions and the chief incentive to individual exertion. The time may come—indeed, there are signs of its approach—when nations will consciously aim at some other than a property career, and individuals will perceive that the purpose of riches is something else than to offer facilities for their further increase or for inglorious ease.

In this devotion to the accumulation of property men have not been led astray by what Shakespeare so magnificently calls—

> "The prophetic soul
>
> Of the wide world, dreaming on things to come."

Material resources are the indispensable requisites to progress. The miseries of poverty are manifest, and there are none greater. The utterly poor man is condemned to servitude and suffering, the woman to degradation. The imperative demands of the animal wants quench the finer elements of character, and the brutal stamps out the human in the desperate struggle for existence.

What wonder that the pauper turns in bestial fury against the rich, who flaunt before him a superfluous luxury? But his passion springs from his ignorance.

Wealth is no longer "spoils," the product of robbery; rather may it be called the reward paid by society for services rendered humanity. It is frequently the booty won in some victory over the elements of nature or of self, and by the practice of those maxims which make men stronger and more useful to those around them. To the possessor it supplies the leisure necessary to the cultivation of his nobler faculties and to the highest of duties—self-development.

The terms "wealth" and "riches" are vague, and to understand the relation of property to personal happiness, which is my present theme, we must define them closer.

The time has gone by when either love is satisfied to live in "a cot beside the hill," or a philosopher in a tub. Both prefer to possess a house in a city street and a cottage by the sea; which is a sign that both the philosophy of love and the love of philosophy have improved. The affectation of despising riches—which never was anything but an affectation—is no longer good form, even among sages.

Let us count what riches give.

The list is short and it is pleasant reading. Riches supply us with the food and drink we like, clothing, shelter, and surroundings to our taste, means of warmth and light, the services and to some extent the companionship of those we choose, and especially leisure and means to pursue our "occupations of choice."

These are the immediate benefits we derive from riches, and practically there are none others. Political economists have therefore called these "real" or "effective" riches, to distinguish them from "potential" or "productive" riches, by which latter they mean property or capital invested with the object of supplying "effective" riches, without personal effort on the part of the owner.

In looking over the list of "effective" riches, one sees that they are all very desirable, and perhaps, I may as well say, essential to personal happiness. I am sure nine-tenths of the civilized world will agree with me. About that, the discussion will be short; but about how to obtain them, that inquiry is not to be disposed of so quickly.

We are now talking business. Let us be practical. *Les affaires avant tout.* Just how much a year do I need to be rich? Here I make an extraordinary discovery, comparable only to that of the Fortunate Isles, where apple trees bore fruits of gold; or the valley of Sinbad the Sailor, where the common pebbles were rubies and diamonds. On urning to that list of "effective" riches, I perceive that very little of it has to do with *things*, and very much of it with *me*. It is based on what *I* like, prefer, choose. If, like the Emperor Nero, I cannot be satisfied with less than peacocks' brains and nightingales' tongues for dinner, I must have the revenues of an empire; but if I am content with bread and beans, with a shanty to keep out the wind and a slop-shop suit for warmth, then a few fifty-cent fees a day—I happen to be a doctor—will make me rich as a Rothschild.

Marvelous discovery! beatific vision! only, at the moment of utmost complacency, calm reflection, like a chill wind, "disencharms the late enchantment." My tastes are not my own. They belong to my parents and my race. I cannot help it that I was born with a thin skin, which requires fine silk next it to be comfortable; with a queasy stomach, that demands delicate dishes; with a thirst for remote and useless learning, which must have expensive books. So from this time forth I flout at and deride that solemn prig of antiquity, whose name I am glad to have forgotten, who taught that there are two ways of getting rich, each equally satisfactory, but one much easier than the other—the one to diminish our wants, the other to increase our incomes. I have no better opinion of his teaching than had Malvolio of the doctrine of Pythagoras, that "the soul of his grandam might haply inhabit a partridge;" and, really, which of the two the antiquated mentor thought the easier I cannot imagine. To me, it has been the latter.

Money, therefore, we must have.

Her physician said of Cleopatra that she had "pursued conclusions infinite, of easy ways to die." The expression might be used of many a modern schemer with reference to getting wealth. But alas! I am afraid, of the thousands of schemes, that of the dry, unimaginative, political economists is the only one worth mentioning; and that is summed up in the hateful word—Economize! or, as they put it in their stiff dialect,—"Diminish the consumption of your 'effective' riches, in order that you may add the surplus to your 'productive' riches, or invested capital."

Some of them are even meddlesome enough to lay down exact rules as to how much one should put aside from an annual income and securely invest, in order to meet the demands of what they call "an enlightened prudence." This, they say, should be one-fourth of such income, and they add that if this with its increment is continued for about five-and-twenty years, the return from your "productive" riches will then be sufficient to supply you with the amount of "effective" riches to which you have been accustomed, without further labor on your part; and you can quietly sit in the chimney corner and live in bliss all the rest of your days, like the prince in the fairy story. This is a page, therefore, good for young married people to read who are starting out in life and have their fortunes to make, and want to "retire" at their silver wedding.

Such slow work will not suit the energetic young man whose determination is to get rich quick and have a good time while he is about it. He has no occasion to go back to antiquity for his two ways of succeeding, and he proposes to use them both as strings to his bow, so that by one or the other he will drive his arrow into the bull's eye of fortune's target. Speculation! Advertising! These are the words of power with which he will enslave the spirits which guard the hidden pots of gold. He is well aware that a bit of red flannel is bait enough for many fishes, and that in angling false flies catch more trout than real ones. The value of knowledge to him is measured by the ability it gives to detect the ignorance of others and to take advantage of it. His plans, like those of Cardinal de Retz, are so laid that, though they fail, they will bring in some return. He will manage to secure a commission even on the expenditures he makes for his pleasures. Such a character, and there are many such in our country, often enough succeeds in his ambitions.

I was in active business for twenty years, and I made the discovery that the excellent precepts which all are taught in infancy and continue to praise in after years undergo certain modifications when it comes to practical life "in the street." Once I amused myself by writing them out as I found them really observed, and I am inclined to insert a few specimens, which I will call

NEW LAMPS FOR OLD.

Not how business should be done, but how others do business, is the proper study.

The brighter your virtues shine, the more fish will be attracted within reach of your gig.

Always praise veracity and honesty; they are useful qualities in others.

The louder you condemn dissimulation, the less you will be suspected of it.

Be virtuous; nothing so enables you to appear superior to those around you.

If you are stingy, do not pretend to be generous; the effort will betray you.

When people express surprise at your meanness, it shows that you must have established a reputation for liberality.

Punctuality is excellent; but the man who comes last to an engagement is the only one who is not kept waiting.

The value of time is its value to yourself.

The simplest device to capture other people's money is to let them think that they can capture yours.

Truth is bright and strong; too bright for most eyes, and too strong to be administered without dilution.

The man who attends the funeral of his own reputation often has a jolly wake.

Marry for love, work for your living; marry for money, work for your liberty.

But enough of these. It will ever hold true that competitive business breeds deception and selfish greed. The business man who pretends otherwise is either a hypocrite or of dull moral sense.

In this race for riches, whether along the peaceful avenue of economy or jostling in the streets of speculation, where comes in the Pursuit of Happiness? Riches, as I have shown, are and can be nothing more than means to this end, and those who, through avarice, greed, or rapacity, make them the end and aim of their aspirations, trade gold for dross. Scarcely less is the error of those who are ever postponing the hour of enjoyment until a certain sum is reached, and their fortune can be rounded off with additional thousands. It is a general tendency in human nature to live in the past or the future, although the present alone is man's. What to him is *now*, and *here*, is all that he can ever possess or enjoy; and if you ask him, he will grant it; but he is driven ever by what seems an irrational and demonic power to seek his joy in what is somewhere else, far off, out of reach, impossible of attainment, beyond his capacities.

The illusive pictures drawn by memory, by hope, and by imagination have their proper place in the palace of Human Happiness; but the majority fix their gaze steadily on these alone, and wander through halls and chambers filled with rich stuffs and costly ware, through corridors looking out on entrancing views and courts opening to the starry heavens, their eyes fixed vacantly on the far distance, and noting nothing of the beauties by which they are surrounded. To waken them by some whisper of what they are missing, and to persuade them to turn their eyes on what is around them, will be my purpose in the chapters immediately to follow.

Bishop Berkeley declared that he was the richest man in England, because he had trained himself to the habit of mind of regarding everything which gave him pleasure as his own. In our days, most philosophers of that school reside in penitentiaries.

The disappointments of the *nouveau riche* are, that what he would like to buy is not on sale, and what he expected to get for nothing, he finds can only be had by paying for it.

That you are rich, is nothing to me; but only whether you are willing to spend your money.

Many strive harder to appear happy than to be so. Ostentation is wealth shamming happiness. Envy is the fool who does not see through the sham.

The rich have less advantage over the poor than the latter suppose.

Not the inventory of your property, but that of your unsatisfied wants, measures your fortune; not your annual income, but your annual deficit or surplus, makes you rich or poor.

After all, the worst of poverty is that it leaves us so little money to give away.

In Grecian legend, the apple of discord was made of gold.

If you teach your son to love money well, you will have such success that he will soon love it better than he does you.

A miser has merry mourners.

Youth saves for age, age for its heirs, and these for nobody.

Do not starve your horse to save your hay.

When you deliver a eulogy on a plutocrat, you had better dwell on his millions than on his methods of getting them.

III. The Pleasures we may Derive from our Senses.

The odious doctrine of the ascetics has been that whatever is agreeable to man is offensive to God; and that to cultivate the pleasurable sensations is to prepare one's self for perdition.

Far more sane than they was that Mohammedan teacher quoted by Gibbon, who, when asked to describe the true believers, replied,—"*They* are the elect of God, whose lives are devoted to the improvement of their own natural faculties."

As mistaken as the ascetics, are those wooden-souled disciplinarians who maintain that we should not look for recreation in our daily work, but put off the thoughts of it to holidays and vacations. These are but one degree better than those hypocrites who will tell you that benevolence should have no place in business, and who will offer you a round sum for a public charity, while they squeeze the salaries of their shop-girls down to the lowest quarter-of-a-dollar.

Down with such imposters! Each hour of our lives is the best hour for enjoying ourselves and for providing others the means of enjoyment; and there is no better way to accomplish both these objects than that suggested by the pious Arab,—"The improvement of our own natural faculties."

These have been divided by experts in such matters into three classes,—the Sensations, the Emotions, and the Intellect. I shall consider the training of each with reference to the special pleasures it can furnish. All are equally worth cultivating. The delights of one are not lower than those of another, if accepted in the proper spirit. He who has right self-culture will derive gratification from them all; and will not be, like the French peasant in Halevy's story, unable to understand how heaven could be attractive unless his native village were transported there.

Some general rules must be respected if the exercise of any of our faculties is to yield the maximum of pleasure. These rules are derived from the physiology of the nervous system; for it cannot be doubted that this underlies, if it is not identical with, every feeling and function of the mind.

I hasten to say this, lest the reader should suppose they are derived from moral philosophy, or based on duty or virtue. I am well aware they could expect a scant hearing were this the case. Men dislike as much to be urged to their good, as to be forbidden what is hurtful. Nor are they difficult to understand; but this helps little; it is easy enough to learn and to teach wisdom; to apply it to our own conduct is what is hard.

The first rule is that of Moderation. Restrain the indulgence in any one pleasure. Immoderation is sure to be followed by exhaustion of the nerve-fibres and subsequent painful reaction. We should not think highly of a gardener who when he picks his flowers pulls his plants up by the roots. Yet this is the fashion in which many men treat their own faculties.

The second rule is that of Variety. Multiply the sources and kinds of pleasure. Increase the susceptibility of all your faculties to its sweet appeals. Seek it in all directions immediately around you. But do not confound the love of variety with instability and freakishness; nor imitate those prodigals who throw the bottle away after the first sip of its contents:—

"Ces buveurs de bière,

Qui jette la bouteille après la première verre."

There are other rules; but to recite them would make this page as dull as a sermon, and it would have as little effect. These two are the chief, and they supplement each other; for he who indulges moderately in all his pleasures will have the capacity to indulge in many, and will preserve those features which are the most desirable in all,—fineness of Quality and persistence of Duration. He will deal with his faculties as a good government with its subjects,—whose aim is not to make a few extremely happy, but to provide for all a fair share of enjoyment, without making any miserable.

The most general sense we possess is that which is called the "muscular" sense. This it is which yields the pleasurable feeling in exercise, in athletic sports, in rowing, riding, dancing, and what old Thomas Fuller called "the descants on the plain air of walking." Through it we gain the sensation of buoyancy and elasticity, we "feel good," our personality is sharpened, and our appreciation of life and what it has to offer is heightened. It is the synonym of healthful activity, and thus becomes the most advantageous preparation for all species of enjoyment.

By physiologists, this muscular sense is not included in the list of "special" senses, because it cannot be localized in any one set of nerves. It is nearest allied to the special sense of Touch, which is centred in certain "tactile corpuscles," distributed irregularly beneath the skin, principally on the finger-tips. They are extremely useful, but not prominently serviceable in the production of pleasurable sensations. The stroking of soft and warm substances, such as velvet and fur, excites agreeable impressions, but they are not very keen. Irritations to the skin are a source of acute annoyance, but their removal affords merely a negatively acceptable condition.

When we consider how slightly most sensations of touch excite subjective states of mind, it is remarkable that in response to one stimulant they are among the most powerful known in nature. This stimulus is that of another personality. The most positive feelings of both aversion and attraction are those excited by physical contact of the naked flesh. This is why it has been accepted in so many countries as a sign and proof of amity. The savage Africans touch noses and the civilized European shakes hands or kisses the hand or the cheek. Such actions are barren conventionalities, unaccompanied by either pleasure or pain; but they are indeed unfortunate who cannot recall any moment of heart's utmost joy and triumph when "the spirits rushed together at the touching of the lips." Such moments are sacred, priceless gifts of the gods, not to be had for gold nor secured by taking thought, so their consideration has no place in this book.

In spite of the active business done at the perfumery counters, the pleasures of the sense of Smell do not seem to come in for a large share of admiration in the modern world. It was different in the days of old. They were considered the most delightful of all, even to Divinity itself. Among the earliest rites of religion was that of burning aromatic incense to the gods; and in the books of Moses good works are described as affording "a sweet savor of satisfaction" to the Almighty. One of the Fathers of the Church speaks of a holy prayer as "the perfume of a just soul" rising to Heaven; and when a good man passed away he was said to die "in the odor of sanctity." Such solemn authorities should justify the cultivation of the pleasures of this sense. They could be supported by abundant quotations from those philosophers, the poets, who have much to say about "the spicy gales of Araby the blest," and other such odoriferous associations.

Some odors are as intoxicating as wine, and others cling to the memory like the impressions of childhood. Yet it is rare for the insane to have delusions of the olfactory sense; and I have found few persons who dream of odors. Some writers who claim to be scientific have set up "a gamut of scents," and others pretend such a harmonic scale can be made the basis of a sort of music of perfumes. This is riding theory beyond sight of practice; but who does not inhale with conscious joy the balsamic fragrance of the pines, the salt and stimulating whiffs from old ocean, or the laden redolence from gardens of roses?

Many writers attribute the pleasure which tobacco gives to its influence on the sense of smell; but this, I am sure, will not explain the intense satisfaction which it yields to men in all climes, consuming it in so many varied ways. I know nothing in physiology more surprising or more puzzling than the eager demand for this plant, which sprang up throughout the world after its discovery in America. I have been a smoker from boyhood, and am just as unable to analyze the pleasure it gives me as to explain it in others.

That prince of epicures, Brillat-Savarin, spent some time in the United States, and in his delightful volume on the *Physiology of the Taste* has a chapter on "cookery in America,"—which is filled with nothing but asterisks and interrogation points!

A hundred years have passed since he was among us, and we have reformed our cuisine indifferently, though not altogether. We have been too much hampered by fatuous bigots preaching that we should eat to live, and not live to eat; whereas we should most certainly live to eat during two or three hours out of every twenty-four; and so doing we shall be passing them more creditably than do most men, or probably ourselves, the remainder of the day. The game of "beggar your neighbor" has advocates enough and fervent disciples, so I shall have something to say about eating for the fun of it and as a fine art.

All nations of culture have connected a certain solemn joy with the act of taking food. To "break bread" with one is the expression of the sweet sentiment of hospitality, and for the lovers to share the same loaf before the High Priest was the simple and beautiful marriage-rite among the ancient Romans. The "love feasts" of the early Christians were the repetitions of the only ceremony which their Founder prescribed; and science traces to appropriate nutrition the growth of both physical and mental abilities. The devout Novalis called meal-times the "flower-seasons of the day," and claimed that all spiritual joys can be expressed through the service of the table. Can there be anything in it unworthy or debasing?

In the light of such declaration should we look on our food-taking, and not merely as feeding and filling. Were the kitchen more of a studio in American homes, we should see a higher style of art in the drawing-rooms. The worst preparation for a day's work is a poor breakfast, and its shabbiest reward is a bad dinner. If our daughters studied more diligently what the Italians call the *melodia* del gusto, their married lives would be attuned to a more harmonious accord.

Consider the appointments and symmetry of a well-served dinner in that high style of art which the French have brought to perfection. The mere sight of the table awakens our esthetic feelings, disperses the cares that have infested the day, and softens the asperities which its rude conflicts have developed. The snowy cloth with its embroidered centre-piece, bearing a vase of roses or restful green; the gay triumphs of the potter's skill, flanked by polished metal and diaphanous crystal, whose varied forms hint of the manifold gifts of the grape; the chairs, so disposed as to suggest how we should live our whole lives—ever near to others, but not jostling them. Then how rhythmical the progress of the repast! the cold, salt shellfish, followed by the hot and spicy soup, harmonized by the neutral flavor of the fish, its creamy sauce relieved by the bare suspicion of the clean acid of the lemon; and so on through the courses, until the aromatic coffee and the tiny glass of liqueur, redolent of wild herbs or of Alpine flowers, remove both thoughts of food and sense of satiety.

The sequence of such a repast is not a conventionality. Medical men as well as epicures know that it is based on physiology. Once, with a friend of like inquiring mind, I ordered a dinner at a restaurant of renown, exactly reversing the usual sequence, beginning with Chartreuse, coffee, and ice-cream, ending with soup, oysters, and hock. The experiment convinced us that the received is the right sequence, and we made no second attempt to put the wrong end foremost.

Many will cry that such a dinner as I describe is one for the millionaire and not for the million. They are in error. In France I have repeatedly partaken of such in families of very humble means. They are, in fact, economical. At an ordinary American dinner I have seen seven vegetables and two meats served at once. Half the number would have set forth a much better repast, if served in the French manner. Moreover, an elaborate dinner is not desirable daily; but to have one, say weekly, is as improving as going to the opera, or listening to a great poet read his own verses.

An essential precept of gastronomic culture is to cultivate a taste for all customary dishes. Every locality has its own. Snails and mussels and cockscombs are favorite dishes in Paris, but I have found few Americans enlightened enough to be willing to like them. A broad taste adds to one's own pleasure and that of others. How disappointing the guest who refuses dish after dish planned with an eye to his pleasure!

Do not be ashamed of the enjoyments of life which are derived from judicious eating and drinking. There are no more accurate standards of a family than its table-manners, table-service, table-talk. Culture is reflected in them as in a mirror. Care not if the bigots and Pharisees call you a wine-bibber and a glutton. You will not be the first to whom they have applied those epithets, and you need not be ashamed of your company. In the city of Paris, where the art of cookery has its home and the Prohibition party no adherents, dyspepsia is scarcely heard of, and the arrests for drunkenness during the entire year of 1890 were—how many, think you?—just thirty-eight!

If I have dwelt with some emphasis on the pleasures of taste, it is because they are little understood in this country and there is a prevalent tendency to decry them. Those which are derived from the sense of Hearing will need no defense. Many of them are matters of constant and intelligent cultivation. We are said not to be a musical nation, but certainly both vocal and instrumental artists are not rare, and those from other countries find among us their most profitable harvest-fields. The intensity and the value of the enjoyment derived from music depend on individual peculiarities which are little modified by cultivation. Of all the exalted pleasures it is the one least communicable and least connected with other faculties. One of the finest pianists in the United States is a negro idiot, and intellectually an appreciative musical audience need not be above him. But I have been told that I have no right to speak about this art. Six generations of Quaker ancestors, who would not permit an instrument of music in the house, have nearly extinguished the musical sense in me.

The music of nature is free to all and intelligible to all. No instruction is demanded to listen with rapture to the blithesome carol of the meadow-lark or the cheery notes of the wood-thrush, joyous denizens of our American fields. The many voices of the wind, now whispering secrets to the pines, now whistling impudently outside our windows, now strident and threatening through the bare branches of winter, bring us messages suited to all moods, and play melodies on our hearts as though their strings were stretched on an Æolian harp. On a sensitive mind the power of these sounds of the wind is altogether peculiar, and appears to be owing to the fact that the agency which produces them is hidden, veiled, and invisible. I would liken it to the effect of distant church bells, heard through the stillness of some Sabbath morn, soft, rhythmical, earnest, inviting us to sweet societies and unseen shrines.

We appreciate too little the delight we almost unconsciously derive from the sense of hearing through the power it gives us to have unrestricted social intercourse in conversation, and to listen to oratory, instruction, and public entertainments. When we observe how even slight deafness circumscribes the life and reduces the number of its sources of enjoyment, we first understand the extent of the gratifications we owe to the faculty of audition, and how important to our happiness are its enjoyment and cultivation.

But how vast is the capacity of man for happiness! How many sources of joy would remain to one deprived of every sense but that of Sight! All his life would not suffice to explore the boundless fields of enjoyment which it alone throws open to him. He has but to cast his eyes around him to revel in the ever-changing garb of earth, in the sky with its majestic clouds sailing across the measureless blue depths, in the splendors of sunrise and sunset, in the transient glory of the rainbow, and in the immortal light of the stars. Stretched on the strand, he may mark the far-off, many-hued, sparkling brine, or elsewhere see great mountains lift their summits to eternal snow and watch them bathed in the rosy glamour of the afterglow, seemingly suspended in mid-air, when night obscures their base.

The beauties of form, line, color, and proportion are open to him, and the treasures of joy which the noble arts of painting, sculpture, architecture, drawing, and engraving have been laboring for thousands of years to enrich the world with in their fullness belong to him. The delicate suggestions of light-and-shade and the inexhaustible fertility of the colorist supply him with storehouses from which he can fill countless hours of gratification. Those elements in our nature which respond to the amusing, the pleasing, the picturesque, and the sublime are almost equally appealed to through the sense of sight; and were we to devote ourselves to answering their fascinating invitations, little leisure should we have left for occupation with any other sense. Nor among these have I enumerated those crowning delights to many minds, the faculty of acquainting themselves with the thoughts of others through reading, and giving perhaps equal pleasure to others by writing, both of which are chiefly conditioned on the sense of sight.

What I have written is but an outline, a scatter of unfinished suggestions, of the numerous enjoyments which we can obtain by the proper cultivation of our senses. Their training, and the rational development of all their functions, are just as essential to our higher life as the cultivation of those which are sometimes, though falsely, called our nobler faculties. There is no aristocracy in the kingdom of nature, and the lowest of our powers, if appropriately directed and educated, is as worthy to occupy the throne as any which in popular repute is deemed the highest.

Sensation is the sense of existence.

There is no "order of excellence" in the faculties of man. One is as excellent as another. The only difference is in the scope of their activities. We should give play to all according to their strength. This is the profound lesson of Walt Whitman's writings.

Sensation, Emotion, Intellect, all three, enter into every action. We should conduct our lives as one plays a game of three-handed euchre, where the two players who are behind constantly enter into combinations against the one who is ahead.

Quaff pleasure in sips, not gulps; let it fall like the manna in the wilderness, a sufficiency daily, not a quantity at once.

Healthy mirth has no reaction. Laughter is lightsome.

Good fare, good manners, good company,—these are the three graces which should preside over the dinner table. Then will the meal include, in the words of Sydney Smith, "Everything of sensual and intellectual gratification which a great nation can glory in producing."

Table-talk,—the best of talk. Even Kant thought it not beneath him to give rules for it: first, of the weather and the roads; next, the current events of the day; then history, art, and philosophy. So did Marsilius Ficinus: first, of divine things; then anecdotes; finally, of art and music.

The unthinking are prone to confine the meaning of Pleasure to Sensation. The coarsest philosophy of life is the most popular, because it is most easily understood, and because it appeals to the universal, which are the merely animal, traits of human nature.

IV. The Pleasures we may Derive from our Emotions.

The emotions are sensations translated into Memory and commented on by the Imagination, with the usual distortion and falsification of the original, characteristic of all translators and commentators.

The primary emotions of Hope and Fear are the recollections of pleasure or pain projected into the future; the disappointment of hope or the realization of fear brings sorrow, regret, or remorse, feelings which are concerned with the past alone.

These reflections suggest how much our happiness has to do with Time. If each could estimate for himself the relative value of the past, the present, and the future, the pursuit of happiness would be a science with results as certain as geometry. As it is, most men pass their days, not in enjoying life, but in getting ready to enjoy it, or in regretting they did not enjoy it; and those who think they are wiser, and who boast that they cultivate the present alone, usually sow it with the seed of thistles and tares to pester their later lives.

The folly of philosophies—and, I may add, religions—has been their effort to divest man of these natural emotions.

"Expect nothing, and you will not be disappointed," is the cheerful advice of the pessimist and the Buddhist; "Fear nothing, for you are in the hands of God," says the Christian fatalist. "Regrets are vain," cries the opportunist;

"live in the present, and let the dead past bury its dead."

In practical affairs, the best philosophy is common sense, which is nothing else than the abstract and epitome of the experience of all mankind through all time; and this arbiter condemns all three of the above maxims as the words of folly and not of wisdom. Hope, fear, and regret are equally necessary to the safe conduct of life with a view to securing the greatest enjoyment from it, and the only point left to consider is the relative extent in which each should be indulged. About this I shall offer a few suggestions.

The skillful architect of his own career will not draw a plan which is either too broad or too high for his means to construct. His hopes will be neither too exalted nor too extended. To be as happy as possible, we must never expect to be extremely happy. Complete happiness is an ideal condition, and we are never farther from the ideal than when we think we have it in our grasp. Nor will his plans be elaborate. The larger the foundation, the more time and money it takes to build the house. The chief enjoyment in life should be drawn from a few, easily accessible sources; though this should not lead us to neglect others that come in our way. One should not refuse a bequest because he has a profitable business. Few understand the limits of their own capacity for happiness. They do not know, as the saying is, when they are well off, and, like a restless inventor, spoil the machine by constantly seeking to improve it. They should ponder on an epitaph on a tombstone in a London churchyard:—"I was well; I would be better; I am here."

Our hopes should not belong to the class called by physicians "incompatibles;" that is, when the realization of one will certainly or probably prevent that of the other. Few errors are more common than this, and few are productive of greater disappointment. Reasonable reflection and ordinary self-knowledge will generally suffice to prevent it. If I set out in life to make a million dollars I cannot expect also to become a distinguished Sanscrit scholar.

The fruition of our hopes should not be placed in a distant future. Life is uncertain, but that is the least objection. What is certain is, that we ourselves shall not be the same next year or next week that we are to-day. Our tastes and moods will change, and it is quite likely that we shall care nothing for the fruit of the plants we are now so diligently cultivating.

This consideration leads up to the last and probably the most useful of all the suggestions on this subject which I shall offer, that is, that in planning for the future, it will, as a rule, repay us best to devote our most earnest and constant attention to the avoidance of pain or misfortune rather than to the preparation of projects of pleasure. We know what we are about when we set to work to forestall a danger or to prevent a disaster; we are by no means so sure as to what course of action will yield us pleasure. The best laid schemes "gang aft a-gley."

Hope and Fear are both deceivers; but we like the company of Hope even when we know she lies; and dislike that of Fear the more, the closer we believe she tells the truth. Many temperaments are tortured more by the dread of misfortune than by misfortune, and are constantly sacrificing the happiness of the present for fear they may not enjoy the future. To such as these would apply the pregnant maxim of Lord Bacon,—"The only thing to be feared is fear."

When in reason and in due proportion to its object, the emotion is salutary and protective. To know what to fear, to take precautions and thus to avoid dangers, are the very conditions of existence. Cowardice is contemptible, but foolhardiness is senseless.

In modern life the most common forms of fear are worry and anxiety. To a certain extent these also are wholesome; there may be good ground for them, and so long as they act as stimulants to healthful activity, they are not to be shirked; but when they lead to morbid states of mind and body, they should be met with appropriate remedies.

The first of these is a deliberate and calm study of the situation and the real causes for fear, if there are any. Spectres lose their terrors by daylight, and most fears are vastly diminished by reflection. What if the worst does come? The worst is never as bad as we imagine it will be. We may also call to mind how useless are many of our anxieties. Why worry about disasters which we cannot prevent? Still less should we worry about those which we can prevent.

When reason and thought will not dispel our fears, we must fight the devil with fire, and conquer one emotion with another. The opponent of Fear is not so much Hope as Courage. Courage recognizes the danger and meets it with a serene front. Confidence in one's powers, the thought of the prize to be won, the love of glory and reputation, a knowledge of the means at our disposal, and a faith in fortune are the considerations which strengthen courage, and if they are marshaled in battle array and led by Enthusiasm, the fears which hovered over our path will be routed like flocks of evil-boding birds.

An easier though less noble escape from fear is Apathy. In different forms it appears as resignation to the will of God, or the inevitable, indifference to results, and philosophic or religious fatalism. An Arab proverb says there are two days on which it is needless to fear death,—the day on which it is decreed we shall not die, and the day on which it is decreed we shall die; and if death need not be feared, what else should be? Modern science is inclined to the doctrine that men's doings are ruled by absolute necessity, and that free will is a delusion. For one, I do not accept the doctrine; but he that does should be released from fear if his logic has any validity.

As the future is clouded with fear and its congeners, so the past is embittered with regret, if not with its gloomier fellows, the pains of contrition and the agonies of remorse. Of all mental misery I have ever witnessed, that of remorse for irreparable injuries done to others was by far the acutest. No one who intimately sees such a spectacle but will learn a lesson which will be a warning for a lifetime. Suicide or insanity is its usual result. But for the lighter forms of regret, reflection on their uselessness, willingness to make reparation, intelligent study of the mistakes of the past as lessons for the future, are remedies which we can always apply with benefit. The keen regret which we feel at our own blunders and shortcomings produces almost a distaste for life. But we may recall the homely business proverb, that he who never makes mistakes never makes anything; and it is something of a satisfaction to think that we did not display the full measure of our capacities in a transaction, but could do it much better had we to do it over again.

The emotions which I have been considering are passive in their nature, and their presence does not markedly influence our external lives. This is not the case with the emotion of Anger, the manifestations of which are primarily external. This is why it is so extremely detrimental to family and social happiness. A person who is choleric, of a bad temper, or an irritable disposition, is heavily handicapped for both the pursuit of happiness and the race for success. I think I have seen more fine prospects ruined by this than by any other single trait; and on the ruins promptly sprang up the weeds of dejection, misanthropy, and moroseness. No other weakness so frequently poisons the joys of married life as a "tempery" disposition. Its control is always difficult, never impossible. The simple precept is, to remain entirely silent and motionless for at least a minute after every flash of anger or sense of irritability. Lord Herbert of Cherbury tells of a splenetic friend of his, whose face would flush almost purple at such moments, but who never broke his self-imposed silence, and therefore never spoke a word which he had to regret. A determined intention to control oneself, and steady practice, will always give such self-mastery.

Anger, when it passes into the chronic form of Hatred, seeks its satisfaction in Revenge. It is rather surprising to find such a calm author as Professor Bain including revenge among the essentials of happiness. In moments of anger the thirst for vengeance is keen, and its gratification pleasant for the time; but from my own experience and that of others whom I have asked, the vengeance which finally appeases long hatred falls far short of affording the gratification we expected, and is even associated with some dissatisfaction with self. The game has not been worth the candle. The satisfaction is greater when our enemy brings ruin on himself through the traits and acts we abhor in him. We can then indulge in an unselfish joy in the spectacle, as did the Israelites when the pride of the Pharaohs was humbled by the consequences of their own arrogance and stiff-neckedness.

The Imagination belongs to the emotional rather than the intellectual faculties, as it has small regard for truth and casts on all things the glamour of that light "which never was on sea or land." Its judicious cultivation adds to the higher enjoyments of life by lifting the events and thoughts of our daily rounds into the mystic realm of the ideal. It is cultivated by the perusal of works of poetry and fiction, and by yielding to the sweet influences of music, song, and the arts of pleasure. In the young it generally needs to be, not so much curbed, as directed in the right road, and in the old to be stimulated. The neglect of it so common in middle life is an unwise preparation for those years which at the best can expect but scant pleasure in watching the mirage of ideal anticipation.

Under the Esthetic Emotions we may class all those which arise from the occupation with what is interesting or beautiful in nature or art. They are perennial fonts of enjoyment to those who will cultivate them in the right spirit—which is, to study them exclusively for the pleasure they yield, and without ulterior aim of utility or didactic purpose. True art acknowledges no allegiance either to utilitarianism or morality—though it is never useless or immoral. Its right aim is to excite within us the consciousness of ourselves by stirring our imagination and feelings into agreeable activity. The emotions which it inspires in the individual rise in value in proportion as they are communicable to others, and thereby develop their contrast to the pleasures of the senses, which are and always remain personal. On the other hand, they differ from those of the intellect by their aim being directed to exciting the faculties which are human. Their limits are defined by these, while the intellect soars far beyond. In the esthetic arts, Man is everything; all refers to him; in science he is nothing, or, at most, a drop in the shoreless ocean of the Universe.

What justice can I render within the limit of a few sentences to the pleasurable emotions excited by the contemplation of Nature? Volumes have been written about and have not exhausted the catalogue of joys offered by the solitary walk through forest and mead, surrounded by that mysterious world in blade and leaf, in bird and insect, in brook and bower, so tantalizingly open and yet so impenetrably closed to our vision. We need no laborious learning, and require no Alps, or ocean, or mighty cataracts, to surcharge our souls with that strange calm and silent joy which Mother Nature ever has ready to pour into the wounds of her returned and wounded sons. A stroll at sunset, through the cow-pasture, by the stream, is all we need, if only our minds are open to the voices and the pictures spread before us. Need I mention the pleasures of gardening, or the charms of the training and companionship of those humbler animals, our pets and favorites, to whose sincerity and affection we so often turn with relief from association with our own species?

Nor shall I go at any length into the obvious pleasure afforded by even a slight acquaintance with painting, sculpture, architecture, photographic reproductions, engraving, those avocations distinctively called by some writers the "arts of pleasure." The very purpose of their creation was to increase the happiness of life, and those who are content to live without understanding and to some extent appreciating what they contribute to human enjoyment, may as well lay down this book at this point, for its whole purpose is alien to them. In some quarters there is a prejudice against these arts; in many more a suspicion that they are frivolous or enervating. Far from it. Goethe, who beyond any other man of this century studied the strengthening of his faculties, recommended that each day we should for at least a few minutes give our minds to the contemplation of some fine work of art or beautiful natural object, were it but a careful engraving, the reproduction of some masterpiece, a pot of natural flowers, or a sunset from our windows. He had found this in his own experience both strengthening and comforting, and none is so indigent or so occupied that it is beyond his reach.

In museums and picture galleries, in the theatre and the opera, in illustrated books and collections of photographs, we have abundant resources to gratify our desire for observing art; and if we wish to share the delights of practicing it, there are the numerous "minor arts," admirably set forth for self-instruction in excellent manuals,—free-hand drawing, water-colors, china painting, embroidery—who can remember all of them?

The finest fruit of the culture of the esthetic emotions, culled from their sunniest sides and served as "human nature's daily food," is what we call "good taste." What an admirable faculty! It is the best of good sense, and walks hand in hand with good manners and good morals. It prunes away exaggerations and affectations, it erases superlatives, it modifies antipathies, and lessens prejudices. The modest home lighted by its fairy lamp shines with a radiance that the luxury of the vulgar plutocrat can never approach. The damsel whose simple garb has been hung by its unfaltering hands will please, when the elaborate toilettes of fashion leave the heart untouched. How much to be envied is the natural possessor of this charming quality! More profitable than envying would be the effort to cultivate it, through the study of the rules of art, the observations of the best models of harmony, and the willingness to accept the opinions of others on subjects where they are acknowledged authorities and to search the reasons on which they are grounded.

The pleasure which we derive from the emotion which is called "Plot-interest" is peculiar and popular. We see it in the avidity with which we follow the adventures of imaginary characters in a novel or drama. It evokes the liveliest sympathy and excitement. Tears follow laughter in quick succession, and with as little real cause. We yield ourselves willingly to the situation, and in the fancied sorrows of the heroine forget our own, which are real.

Akin to those of plot-interest are the Emotions of Pursuit, which impart such zest to hunting, fishing, and allied sports. We care little for the quarry; a "paper chase" is almost as exciting as a lion hunt; but it is the sense of the self-conscious and strenuous exertion of our faculties which gives us the enjoyment. This explanation may not be obvious in the case of the enthusiastic angler, who sits by a dull canal under an umbrella all the afternoon, satisfied with a few gudgeons; but this enthusiasm makes up for the lack of positive exertion.

More obscure is the intense and absorbing pleasure which most derive from the Emotions of Risk, which are excited by games, especially those of chance, or where skill is so equally balanced that chance comes in for a large share of the result. This is pre-eminently the emotion which most men cultivate in their hours of recreation. Billiards, chess, pool, cards, backgammon, horse-racing, athletic games, and personal contests, where the opponents are as equally matched as practicable, make up to most minds the definition of Enjoyment. The various games of cards offer the most favorable types of games, as when played fairly and well they have a large and constant element of chance. They have been in ill odor, as being the most convenient means for gambling. But to the one who really enjoys the emotions of risk, the stakes are subordinate. Any one who appreciates the charms of a rubber of whist, or the agreeable exercise of a game of billiards, will not want the additional and often unpleasant addition of a stake, and those who fail to appreciate, or neglect to cultivate, these emotions as a source of pleasure in life, deprive themselves of that which would cheer many a sad hour by innocent and healthful employment.

When I glance back at what I have written, I see I have done little more than catalogue, and that incompletely, the sources of enjoyment offered by the Emotions. But if this superficial survey developed such possibilities, how much of the pure gold of joy awaits the careful prospector who will follow the veins and sift the sands of the region thus thrown open to his energies?

There is this peculiarity in both works of art and scenes of natural beauty, that they impress us most vividly in periods of deepest dejection or highest elation, and are thus incomparable aids in restoring mental equilibrium.

The painful, the hideous, and the shocking are legitimate inspirations of art, as well as the beautiful and agreeable. The latter intimate the direction we should go, the former the dangers we may have to encounter and the existence of suffering which calls for our sympathy.

Fear and Folly are the couple whose offspring is Distress.

The emotion that does not incite to action, enfeebles.

Activity does not mean excitement. Healthful action is uniform. The wheel of most rapid revolution is the most regular in its motion.

Nature soothes because she knows nothing of our conflicts. Like Spinoza's God, she loves no one and hates no one.

Not nature, but nature's infinite analogies, are what quicken the heart and supply it with endless interpretations of its own experiences.

The sombre, the desolate, and the vast in nature appeal most strongly to the educated spirit, because they typify what is measureless, and therefore mournful, in its aspirations.

V. The Pleasures we may Derive from the Intellect.

When I speak about billiards and fishing and opera-going as pleasures, I am sure everybody understands me. But now that I have to refer to the enjoyment derived from study and thinking and scientific research, I fear the majority will prepare to stifle their yawns or skip the chapter.

Yet I have heard of, and even known, men who turned to such occupations for their highest felicity, and counted such joys above gold or lust or glory or love,—because enemies might rob them of these, but never of the treasures of the understanding. The one aim of their lives was the Search for Truth; and to them all truths seemed equally great, equally worthy devotion. One spent years in the study of polyps and fungi, and by them learned to explain the laws which have developed man and mind; another neglected his profession in order to investigate the anatomy of a worm, and made a discovery which restored thousands of his fellow-beings from wretched invalidism to happy health.

Such exceptional beings are not to be set up as the pole stars for all mariners over life's ocean. A man cannot be happy beyond the tastes and faculties which he has; and it is as absurd to expect all to enjoy equally the pleasures of the intellect as it would be to look for all to be pleased with the flavor of the same dish. Every man, however, who is not idiotic or insane possesses an intellect, and can derive a great deal of pleasure from its cultivation; and it is always to some degree in his power to cultivate it in the right manner.

If he only knew the many advantages of these pleasures he would not fail to give them his attention. Almost alone of enjoyments they leave behind them no sense of exhaustion, no painful reaction or regrets. They are as varied as our moods, suited as well to assuage our sadness as to prolong our cheerful moments. At no period of the year are they out of season, age does not wither them, nor does "custom stale their infinite variety." They are social or solitary as we choose to make them, and they know no sense of satiety, as with them the appetite grows by what it feeds on. They flatter our self-complacency by showing us that we are growing wiser, and they stir within us sympathy and appreciation for others. They are always at hand, for the appreciative student carries between the covers of his Shakespeare more pleasure than the millionaire can stow in his yacht. Finally, and as the clinching argument in their favor, they are economical, doubly economical, for they cost little or nothing, and they save us many a broad piece which we should have had to spend for pleasures gratifying the senses the same length of time; economical also of our lives, for the student class are those who have the greatest longevity.

Especially would I urge women to pursue intellectual pleasures rather than those of the emotions, to which they are now largely confined. Some of the most promising marriages fail through lack of intellectual sympathy in the wife. How sad it is to read these words of John Stuart Mill in his essay on the liberty of women,—"Young men of the greatest promise generally cease to improve as soon as they marry;" a result which he attributes directly to the absence of sympathy in their wives for that which constitutes the highest culture, and often a direct opposition to it. His opinion is valid everywhere, though it should be true nowhere. For the sake of her husband and her children, she should resolutely turn to the cultivation of her mind as one of the firmest holds on their affections.

One of the simplest forms of intellectual pleasure is that which is derived from riddles, puzzles, conundrums, and rebuses. Children and primitive nations are especially captivated by these agreeable stimulants to their ingenuity. In French country towns they are highly popular, and many of the cafés have cercles who meet nightly to solve the enigmas proposed in the weekly papers and forward the solutions to the editor. Those which are successful receive a small prize or an honorable mention. The placid bourgeois appear to derive extraordinary enjoyment from this pastime.

Most people understand "cultivating the intellect" to mean reading. Sometimes it has this result, but generally it is too desultory, miscellaneous, and aimless. Were it directed to a more definite purpose it could be made to yield more profit and more enjoyment. I do not mean to the purpose of instruction, as probably the reader has been in haste to suppose, but so as to endow the mind with a wider range of interests and thus with more sources of pleasure.

Read what interests you and interest yourself in what you read—that is the best rule. I have a small opinion of lists of the "hundred best books," or courses of reading cut and dried for you by large societies. They may instruct, as do lessons appointed by a master; but I am speaking of reading for pleasure; and really that is the only kind worth mentioning. I have always liked reading, but I never could bear to lay out a course for myself, still less follow any proposed by another.

My own very satisfactory plan has been like that of the prospector for minerals. He wanders aimlessly over the mountains till he finds the sign of ore; then he ceases his roving and traces out the vein with zeal and patience. You read an article in a magazine; on one point mentioned you would like further information. Do not pass it by and forget it, but go to the encyclopedia or the library and follow it up; it will lead you to two or three volumes, not to be read, but to be consulted; these will start several allied points of interest; look them up in the same manner; and before you know it you will be burrowing for hours among books with the greatest delight.

By adopting this plan you not only pursue the bent of your own inclination and follow your own fancies, but without knowing it you are obeying some of the most scholastic rules for reading laid down by the learned.

One of these is to "distribute the attention;" by which they mean to learn to pass easily from one subject to another. Do not become so absorbed in one line that others have no charm for you. This is a common error with students of specialties. The great Darwin regretted that toward the close of his life his unremitted attention to science had destroyed his power of appreciating poetry and the drama. Yet neither should one hurry from book to book, or from topic to topic. Each should be pursued up to the point of commencing fatigue; then the volume should be laid down, and an effort made to recall the main facts we have read, and arrange them in order in the mind. What looks like desultory reading will not remain desultory long if pursued in accordance with these suggestions.

As to what kind of books to read, the brief answer is, all kinds. Variety is the guiding principle. Do not read in ruts. Some say we should always have some main theme to which others should be subordinate. The advice is good for those who have by nature some such leading interest; only for them it is unnecessary; and for those who have not, I believe it is useless, for such an interest can rarely be created by the will. I doubt if one can say off-hand,—"From this out, my chief interest shall be in the history of Ancient Egypt," or something of that kind. Disraeli once remarked that biography has a greater interest than history, because it is life without theory; and French writers are better than English, because they have fewer ridiculous ideas of life. Some such plea could be entered for every department of literature, and each would be just. Unquestionably, the tendency at present is to read too exclusively works of the imagination, novels, romances, dramas, and the like; the pleasure they yield is ephemeral and is apt to disqualify for that which is more persistent though less intense, derived from works based on objective realities.

For one branch of literature I must, however, put in a special claim, as it has been such a pleasure to me ever since I learned to read, and that is Poetry. I have heard it sometimes said that this is a taste of youth, and dies a natural death with advancing years. My own experience is quite the contrary. The delight we derive from accurate rhythm, melodious words, fine thoughts, and the depicting of deep emotions, ought to increase as our experience of the world and wider learning make us more familiar with them. This has been the result in my own case and in that of others whom I know or have heard of; for instance, Sir Henry Holland, writing his biography when about eighty years of age, lays stress on the enjoyment the study of the poets continued to afford him; and my mother, at eighty, derived much pleasure in committing to memory and repeating new poems. There is a sense of completeness, of perfection, which is given a fine thought by appropriate expression in rhythmical language, which prose can never equal, and which, through the potent magic of Form, lifts the mind out of the material into the ideal world, and grants us a momentary glimpse of the Infinite.

If we do not recall to mind and think over what we read we lose most of the pleasure and all the profit of the action. This was what the English philosopher Hobbes meant when he said,—"If I had read as many books as some men, I should be as ignorant as they." To read without reflecting is like buying grain for food and never grinding it. Through reflection on the images, incidents, and forms of expression with which reading has stored the memory, the highest enjoyment from the process is secured. The mind, like the body, is maintained in a state of pleasurable activity, not by what it swallows, but by what it digests and assimilates. Many people, however, are like dear Charles Lamb, who artlessly confessed,—"I cannot sit and think—books think for me;" and if they think for all to such good purpose as they did for him, no one could complain.

In fact, reflection, meditation, though its pleasures have been chanted by poets and sages for thousands of years, is probably that form of intellectual activity which is least admired and least desired of any. It is not the same as "studying out a subject," or exerting the creative faculty, as an inventor when he is devising a machine; but the leisurely calling up from our memory of its various contents. They may be from reading or from conversation or from our experience of life. We may present these to ourselves as the pictures of a gallery or as the scenes of a drama or as a series of connected events; and we may endeavor to discern what relations they bore to each other, or speculate on what would have been the results had they occurred differently, or not at all. We may renew half-forgotten pleasures, or smile at useless pains, or recall long since vanished woes. Lessons for our guidance or knowledge of ourselves may unexpectedly come to us as the results of such self-communing; or we may cast our eyes to the future, and enjoy in prolonged anticipation those pleasures which may never come, or, if they come, can last but a moment. This is the nature of that reflection which, if we learn it and cultivate it, will enable us to pass many a pleasant hour, when otherwise we should be cut off from all sources of amusement, as in some dreary waiting for a train or enforced and lonely vigil.

As solitude is thus relieved by exercise of our minds, society by the same may have many an added charm. What a fund of rational enjoyment is offered by reading circles, debating societies, literary coteries, and associations for the purpose of studying Shakespeare or Browning or Ibsen, or whatever other literary star may be in the ascendant! There are some pretentious persons who profess to be above such gatherings. They can well be dispensed with in them. The tendency to be guarded against in order to make such schemes prosperous is that of improving the mind. This should be entirely incidental and secondary. When one joins a dining club, he expects a dinner which he likes, not a special diet prescribed by his medical adviser; and so it should be with literary clubs. Let the improvement take care of itself. It will do so.

Alongside of reading and reflection we must place writing. Many will need no explanation why this should be classed among the pleasures of life; while to others it is always a distasteful drudgery. They escape it whenever possible, and reduce it to its lowest terms, which means letter-writing—and in their case always the writing of very middling letters. A letter, indeed, is a great tell-tale, and tells the more the less it says. A score of years in editorial work, during which the competency of numerous writers had to be gauged by some quick standard, taught me that the letter of transmittal is generally enough to decide on the merits of the manuscript offered. To him who can appreciate its revelations there is no more infallible test of general culture than an ordinary letter.

Correspondence by some is classed among the lost arts. As an art, we can let it go; but as one of the most agreeable of pleasures, it will ever remain. Nature, not art, is what gives it its charm. The free expressions of personal feelings, thoughts, and observations, the intimacy and confidence which we can never find in books or magazines, the household words and pet phrases which grow up between correspondents, the tacit assumptions of common tastes and knowledge, these are what endow correspondence with its boundless charms for those who cultivate it.

Some writers have extolled the pleasure to be derived from keeping a diary. They claim it gives one much delight to turn back to an accurate record of what he did or heard or saw at a given period of his past life. They add that it is also a judicious habit for our own well-being, teaching us what errors we have made, what false opinions harbored, what aims pursued fruitlessly, and the like. I believe what these writers say, and commend their advice to those for whom it is suited. As for myself, I never could follow it. The diaries which I have occasionally begun, I have usually ended by throwing into the fire. It seems to me a man must either progress very little, be supernaturally wise to begin with, or have incredible self-complacency, to read with satisfaction a diary of his own five years old which contains anything but the most naked facts. Amiel's diary is one of the most attractive published of recent years; but it certainly could have been no pleasure to his sensitive mind to have renewed its sorrows by perusing its morbid reflections.

I have left to the last the consideration of the highest of all intellectual joys,—the Pursuit of Truth. This should be the aim of every thought, and the sole, conscious occupation of our understandings. As our senses are satisfied only with pleasure, in like manner our reason finds no rest until it attains to what is true. That man is useless on the face of the earth, and wastes his life, who devotes his time to anything else than the pursuit of happiness or the search for truth.

They are not antagonistic. They are compatible one with the other; perhaps they are identical, when both are clearly seen and correctly understood. That great teacher who rejected the narrow prescriptions of asceticism, and came eating meat and drinking wine, also taught that the one comforter, the Paraclete, which should in future ages complete the happiness of man, is "the Spirit of Truth."

There need be no discussion as to what Truth is, nor need we, like jesting Pilate, make the inquiry and "stop not to hear reply." The answer is as clear as it is brief. Truth is that which will bear constant and free examination. Renewed observation, verification, re-examination, investigation—whatever is true will bear all these without diminution of its lustre; and any statement which men advance as true, but are unwilling to submit to these tests, they know is more or less of a lie.

The highest and clearest truths are to be found in the physical and natural sciences. The latter especially offer unending pleasant vistas to those who can interest themselves in them. The passion of collecting in natural history is a rich source of enjoyment, inexpensive, always open, exhaustless in extent. Whether it be minerals, plants, insects, coins, weapons, or what not, their accumulation occupies vacant hours and they furnish abundant materials for thought, reading, study, and conversation. The man who has a cabinet stocked by his own efforts is one who never complains of ennui. The day for him is never too long.

As for the devotees of Science, there is no need for me to inform them of the pleasure they derive from its pursuit. They are too well acquainted with its joys, transcending any which wealth or popular renown can offer, to care to read their eulogy. But this intense devotion must be born with one or date from some early association, and can rarely be acquired in mature years, so that it need not be dwelt upon here.

"Life according to reason,"—this was Aristotle's definition of happiness.

The intellect is cold because it is unsympathetic. We must cultivate with it the imagination, which by vividly portraying pain, develops sympathy.

Do you wish to improve your mind? Then read carefully what you do not understand, and listen dispassionately to what you do not agree with.

Error is more agreeable than truth, because the latter points out our limitations and the former conceals them.

An error actively advocated is healthier than a truth lazily accepted. Thought becomes fecund only in action.

A mistake is sooner corrected than a falsehood, because it is nobody's interest to maintain it.

Novel-reading is the fashionable narcotic; opium, chloral, and hasheesh together count fewer victims.

All that is, is a prophecy of what will be; hence, to a philosopher, the chief interest in things is their symbolical value.

Vivre caché, c'est vivre heureux. This was Descartes' motto. It should be translated: "To be able to retire with pleasure to your own thoughts, is to be happy."

What is the pleasure of being famous? That of being talked of by those you do not know, who do not know you, and in whom you take no interest.

VI. The Satisfaction of the Religious Sentiment.

After all, the only standard of value which we need apply to anything is the amount and quality of Happiness it yields. This alone can concern Man anywhere and at any time. His religions should be measured by no other mete-yard. All were created by man, for the happiness of man; though all claim another, a superhuman, origin, and pretend to bear the sign-manual of the Divine.

They are right, and what seems a paradox is a sober fact. As much the productions of human hands and brains as are the robes and paintings in which they are bedecked, they have something in them which no externals can represent, and which lifts them above their material drapery. Human beyond all else that man has devised, for that very reason they are superhuman.

The strange law of Evolution is, that nothing in nature reaches its perfection but by becoming something else. The species in attaining its utmost development is transformed into another species. Man would not be the noblest product of the earth did he not feel himself too noble for it; did not the presage and aura of a higher destiny forever float around his thoughts, making themselves felt at the moments of the utmost tension of his faculties; as when behind the parapet of Chillon one rises on extreme tip-toe, and catches a glimpse of the glittering lake and massive Alps beyond.

The vital principle, the motive power, which has created and maintained all religions is the Ideal of Humanity. Each age has had its own, each individual has his own, no two the same. Creeds and churches do but formulate and endeavor to materialize the average conceptions of a period or a class; but their labor is vain. Rejecting the old, putting on the new, the race marches forward to loftier ideals, the milestones of its progress being the wrecks of temples and the ruins of churches. Religions rise and fall and disappear; but Religion grows forever, because it is the inseparable associate, aye, the very expression, of that mysterious impulse on which man's future development depends, and which makes him part and parcel of the infinite Energy in which he lives and moves and has his being.

Time and Truth will reconcile all religions; but the time will be long and the truth will be slow to make its way. The schools of dogmatic doctrine claim to have embalmed in a creed and confined in a code the whole truth necessary for the happiness of man; not perceiving that they are like children to whom a magician hands a box in which he seems to have shut a pigeon; they open it cautiously, to discover that it is empty, and he points to the bird soaring up to the sky. Only they take good care not to open the box. Their schools and teachers resemble those feeble-minded folk who imagine they increase in knowledge by constantly talking to themselves.

Always boasting of their devotion to truth, they steadily repudiate it. That alone is true which will bear repeated, free, and unbiased investigation; but dogmatists cry,—"Never discuss your faith; never doubt your creed; for he that doubteth is damned." What progress they make is not from within, but is forced on them from without by the free spirit of inquiry; and what they thus unwillingly accept, they audaciously claim as the product of their own efforts. Everywhere the spirit of ecclesiasticism is the secret or open foe of strict and complete veracity; and yet no permanent alleviation of the sufferings of mankind can come except from veracity. And from this it will come. No matter what the weather is, this seed is sure to grow.

What unspeakable unhappiness religions have brought on the race! Altars dripping with the blood of human victims, mothers casting their babes into the fires of Moloch, teachers crucified by the rabble whom they sought to instruct, millions perishing between the Crescent and the Cross, hideous chambers of the Inquisition, Bruno burning alive in Catholic Rome, and Legate in Protestant London,—a thousand such historic events would give no notion of the miseries which religions have inflicted on mankind, and continue to inflict.

Worse than these have been their blighting breath on individual minds, darkening them with terrors of the supernatural, with racking doubts, despair, and madness; destroying the natural and beautiful growths of the affections; frowning on the attractions of the arts of beauty; crushing the desire of knowledge and the love of investigation; urging men in the ignoble egotism of self-salvation to sacrifice their own happiness and that of those nearest and dearest to them. These influences still exist; they are ever in the spirit of clericalism and dogmatism, and are restrained from plunging mankind again into the dark ages only by that higher and real religion which acknowledges neither form nor creed nor dogma, but only the might and right of Truth and Love.

I would ask what teachings do religions—and I have those in mind which are prevalent in civilized countries to-day—impart, which in any way compensate for the enormous unhappiness and intellectual degradation thus caused?

Most sects calling themselves Christian will at once reply that the happiness they promise is not of this world but of the next, and that he who looks for enjoyment here will forfeit it hereafter. Yet when the evidence for this daring statement is asked for, not an iota can be offered on which there is unanimous concurrence among the sects themselves.

What they do offer, and what gives them their real control over men's minds, may be summed up as follows: A belief in the Divine government of the world and the paternal care of God over each believer in Him; greater cheerfulness in the acceptance of the misfortunes of life as the wise and ultimately beneficent decisions of His will; an expectation of a life after death; the hope that sins will be forgiven; and the improvement in morals which follows these convictions.

These are undoubtedly valuable aids to human happiness. The question is, what part of them belong to Religion and what to religions; in other words, will not the religious sentiment itself, freed from the shackles of dogmatic belief, yield to man all the happiness offered by sectarian doctrines, relieved of the misery to which they condemn him? When I think of the mental agony caused in millions of lives by the pictures of hell, of eternal damnation, of the last judgment, and of a cruel and merciless God, which most Christian teachers hold before their congregations, I long for the time predicted by that apostle of the new life, Giordano Bruno,—"When the gods shall lie in Orcus, and the dread of everlasting punishment shall vanish from the world."

Reason has no conflict with religion. Science is based on the assumption that the order of the Universe is one of intelligence, and of an intelligence identical with ours. All force is directed by reasoning energy, which means that it is purposive. Why seek further? Call it Energy or Force or God, the thought is the same.

Whether that share which we possess in the energy of the All remains in personality after physical death, what dogma can prove? what science deny? Enough that in the beautiful words of the burial service of the Protestant Episcopal Church, we are justified in retaining "a reasonable and holy hope" that the victory of the grave is not eternal. Should it be so, what is the dread of it but a delusion of the imagination, which pictures non-existence as felt in non-existence?

The sense of sin, the story of the fall and its expiation by a divine sacrifice; is it not strange that no one word that this was His mission escaped the lips of Him who is said to have been the willing victim? The notion of sin as taught in dogmatic belief has no existence in the unwarped mind nor in scientific psychology. Men are involved in a chain of cause and effect from which they have little chance of escape; and even human justice revolts at administering punishment for involuntary acts. *Tout comprendre, c'est tout pardonner;* that infinite Mind, which sees before and after, asks the blood of no victim to understand and to pardon the blind gropings of the wretched children of men.

What abuse has been made of the doctrine of Faith! Its upas-shade has harbored the grossest growths of superstition. Faith is either laziness or cowardice. We accept the opinions of others to save ourselves the trouble of forming our own, or to escape the pains of doubt. But doubt is painful only to him who accepts on authority, not to him who honestly seeks, truth through the efforts of his own powers.

But piety, morality, how can these be secured without dogmatic religions? This is the answer so often hurled as final in their defense. The history of sectarianism shows anything but a clean bill of morality, as I have already hinted; if there is any one corner-stone to the edifice of ethics, it is the honest pursuit of verifiable truth, and that no dogmatic religion dares to advocate. History shows that every great reformer of the morals of his day has been called a schismatic by the Churches.

The arch error is, however, not in these directions, but in the universal assumption that the moral life, that piety, is the chief end of man and an object in itself. Nothing of the kind. The moral law neither exhausts nor completes the nature of man. It is but one strand in the many-fibred thread of his existence; and to suspend his whole life and destiny from this will always, as it always has in the past, lead to the fall and the destruction of his noblest aspirations. Piety, a devout morality, the culture of the religious sentiment, these are only some and far from all of the means and steps to the highest culture of the individual life.

They are not individual in the sense that their culture can be successfully conducted in solitude or by mystical meditation. True religion never isolates, but unites. Not the happiness of himself in another world, but the happiness of others in this, is the aim of the true believer. From theirs, he derives his own. The "Communion of Saints," the "Congregation of the Righteous," the "Society of Friends,"—these are the expressions which indicate the direction of the religious sentiment in unimpeded activity. In such "solemn troops and sweet societies," it yields that joy to man which his nature is capable of receiving only in its highest moments of exaltation, and which it would be sad to think he could ever be deprived of.

But this we need not fear. A religion that is not afraid of free investigation, but courts it; one that dismisses the supernatural because it recognizes that no law can be higher than that of nature; whose maxim is the utmost veracity in thought and action at all costs; whose aim is to produce as much visible happiness and to prevent as much misery as possible; which binds men together through united sympathies for these aims; which constantly prompts to healthful and fruitful activity; which is truly an inspiration, and sanctifies by its presence the equally true inspirations of the highest art and the purest science; and whose clearly recognized purpose is to promote the ideal perfection of humanity as represented in the individual man;—this is the Religion of the Future, and one that the future will not allow to perish.

The aim of science is the Real; of art, the Ideal; of action, Happiness. It is for religion to unite this trinity into a unity in each individual life.

Man's highest efforts in art or thought or life are in themselves religious, because they represent elements in the better future life of the race. This is what Michael Angelo meant when he said, "Who strives after perfection in Art, strives after something Divine."

The divine is not the superhuman, but the ideally human. The infinite must become incarnate to be intelligible. It is so in all great religious acts and works.

The ideally true is the potentially true.

Physical science is opposed to both religion and metaphysics, and yet is forever attracted toward them; because, struggle as it may, in them alone can it find its own completion.

The religious sect that condemns reason, condemns itself; and the latter sentence is the only one which will be executed.

The poetry of science will be the inspiration of the religion of the future.

Were there a religion other than human, it could not appeal to humanity.

The human cannot get along without the divine in some form. The least religious men, such as gamblers, are the most superstitious. As Novalis says, "Where the gods are not, ghosts take their place."

The aim of classic religions was the salvation of the State; of Christianity, the salvation of certain individuals, the Elect; of the religion of the future, the salvation of the whole race of man.

A religious doctrine should compel belief, like a theorem in geometry. Most doctrines are accepted because their believers know too much to disturb their tranquillity by examining them, or too little to comprehend them.

As in dreams the impressions of childhood continue to recur, so in modern religions conceptions belonging to the childhood of the race are still urged upon us.

The dogmatists prefer to frame rules, rather than give reasons; because the latter will be judged on their merits, while the former are accepted on authority.

Half-true is harder to refute than wholly false. The defenders shield themselves behind the part that is true. Not the mud at the bottom, but the stain in the water, clouds the stream. This is why numerous sects continue to survive, perpetuating many errors by means of a few truths.

There is something comical in a man making a business of religion, levying a charge on this world for his services to the next. The Quakers must have had a vein of humor in their opposition to all sorts of paid priests.

The priests of the Church of the Future will be the spiritual leaders of their generation, those educators, poets, scientists, physicians, journalists, and others, who practice their avocations with a view to the interests of others as well as their own.

Eating your dinner is as sacred as saying your prayers, and making your living is as noble as dying for your faith.

I heard Walt Whitman once say that life without immortality would be like a railroad train made up entirely of engines. The forces of individuality seemed to him too mighty, to conceive as possible their limitation to this world.

The spirit of Christ's teachings is too democratic to be in hearty sympathy with either science, philosophy, art, or the pursuit of pleasure.

Piety is sometimes merely the last passion; sometimes merely the last fashion.

The devout are the disappointed.

Prayer refreshes and relieves the mind by strengthening the confidence, by diverting the thoughts, and by admonishing the soul of higher themes. The Jew prays to Jehovah, most Christians to the Virgin or the Saints, the Buddhist to himself; all are consoled and benefitted; equally so is he who meditates on the laws, the life, the love, and the power, manifested in the universe of matter and mind around him.

VII. The Cultivation of Our Individuality.

When you tell a person that he resembles so-and-so, he is always surprised. He does not see the slightest similarity. Were he to meet his double in the street, he would pass him without recognition. It would be the same with his mental counterpart; in fact, most men are so slightly acquainted with themselves, and are so lost in the crowd, that they no longer know the way home. They are merely composite photographs of the people they have met. Unconscious actors, they speak the words and imitate the feelings of those around them until they lose the cue of their own proper parts.

This deplorable lack of Individuality is the fruitful cause of many a failure and much unhappiness. It arises from a lack of self-knowledge, self-confidence, and self-respect, and is constantly leading men astray in their plans of life.

The complaint is often made that men deceive each other; but they deceive themselves far more. They imagine they have talents which they do not possess, and overlook those which are their own; they attempt what is beyond their powers, and allow those they have to rust through want of use. They believe that is their own which they have but borrowed, and go forth to till imaginary fields, leaving their own garden-plots lie fallow.

How much better to live one's own life, to be oneself, to cultivate what abilities we have rather than to waste time on those we have not, to learn the limits of our own capacities and insure success by working within them! The advice of the sages of all times has been to swear by the words of no teacher, to call no man Master, to think our own thoughts, to be true to ourselves, to make our own felicity, and not to run about the world trying to share that of others by aping their sentiments and actions.

The greatest teachers have not desired disciples, but friends. They have never exerted authority, and where they could not persuade or convince, they have sought no proselytes. To them the independance of the individual mind has been of more importance than the dissemination of any article of faith or element of instruction. Spinoza, Herder, Wilhelm von Humboldt, our own Emerson, have all in spirit joined with Goethe in singing that the secret of the highest happiness of man rests in the preservation of his own free personality:—

Höchstes Glück der Erdenkinder

Sei nur die Persönlichkeit.

Peer in this august company, deeper than any in his devotion, speaking at every hazard, I name my late friend, Walt Whitman, the "singer of one's self," "chanter of Personality," "self-balanced for all contingencies," holding creeds and schools in abeyance, ceasing not till death.

The man of independent mind and strong personality is never trivial or vulgar, no matter what his education or social position. The artist who plays solo commands our attention. The plant which is indigenous is alone strong and hardy; exotics are starvelings. Individuality is contagious, and it is bracing and stimulating to meet such a character. His presence is a benefit to a whole company, and a company of such is worth a regiment of nonentities. The richest agricultural community I ever saw was in France, where every peasant cultivated his own little field; and the poorest was in our own country, where every man was trying to feed his cattle on somebody else's range.

The latter theory, however, is that which is popular to-day. Dreamers are constantly devising schemes by which the idle and incompetent may live off the proceeds of the diligent; labor unions deprive their members of the liberty of speech and the liberty of work; socialism would reduce all to a common level; syndicates and trusts break down individual enterprise; sectarian colleges limit their calls to professors who will echo their tenets; and thus in all directions the free growth of the individual is hemmed in by the hedges of prejudice, tradition, creed, and false theory.

Many people scarcely know what Individuality is. They think it means to wear a straw hat in winter, or in some other way to make oneself conspicuous. This is precisely what it does not mean. The man who is himself is always simple and natural; he buys his hat at the hatter's and allows the tailor to make his clothes. To act otherwise is affectation and singularity, not individuality. Simplicity is a charming characteristic of the strongest minds. It is recorded of Sir Isaac Newton that he was not distinguished from other men by any peculiarity, either natural or affected; upon which Dr. Johnson makes the excellent remark,—"Newton stood alone merely because he had left the rest of mankind behind him, not because he deviated from the beaten path." Those who met Robert Browning for the first time were agreeably surprised to find the great poet was in ordinary society simply a gentleman. All forms of affectation are confessions that we are not what we pretend to be, and are inconsistent with true individuality.

Nor is it obstinacy and self-assertiveness, as others suppose. The man who aims to be himself will wish others to remain themselves, and will be the last to obtrude his personality in a disagreeable way upon them. Obedience, voluntary subjection to the will of others, is part of his self-training. He who cannot obey, cannot command. Nor is he one who lives for himself, is solitary or selfish. The characters who in history shine with the most marked individuality have been those who moved most actively among their fellow men.

True individuality is that confidence in self which arises from a knowledge of one's own powers, their extent and their limitations. This knowledge can be obtained only by experience, by testing the powers, and by gauging their strength in the contest of life.

From how many vexations does a correct estimate of our capacities free us? Envy, disappointed ambition, premature exhaustion, disgust of the world, these arise from inadequate notions of our own abilities. On the other hand, that life has always a large share of happiness which is spent in the prosecution of some object to which our faculties are equal, and which therefore we prosecute with success.

In judging of our own powers we are just as likely to under- as to over-estimate them, and the results are equally painful.

How acute are the sufferings of a diffident, shy, self-distrustful, over-sensitive disposition! Such a temperament is a sad make-weight in the struggle of life. More men fail through ignorance of their strength than through knowledge of their weakness. They are like a farmer, who gathers scanty harvests all his life from fields covering rich deposits of ore, which, did he but work them, would enrich him. The fear of falling often hinders from climbing.

Let such remember that few score success, but after failures. Few experiences are indeed more painful than to devote ourselves earnestly to an undertaking and discover that it is beyond our powers; but the failure teaches us the extent of our strength and increases it for the next effort. We can never learn our own abilities but by trying for what is beyond them; like the athlete, who lifts heavier and heavier weights until he reaches those which he cannot move. Practice and persistence are strong cards. "Time and I," said Philip II, "against any other two."

Much of our sensitiveness, did we but know it, springs from concealed vanity. We covertly fear that if we display our powers it will give others the opportunity to take their measure; and this we mistrust will not prove favorable to us. But there is a consolation in view. We may call to mind that as the best of authors do not escape censure, so the poorest do not lack admirers.

The over-estimation of one's faculties leads to vanity and self-conceit, traits not generally painful to the individual, and not so injurious as excessive diffidence. It does a youth no harm to believe that he was born to perform great deeds. It is easier to cut back rank shoots than to fertilize sterile roots. He who is confident that he can leap beyond the mark, will be pretty certain to reach it. Attrition with the world usually reduces vanity to its proper limits. Disappointed ambition is bitter, but some bitters are excellent tonics.

That individuality is genuine which is confidence in self, based on knowledge of self.

Nowhere does it show its worth more than when it comes into contact with Opinion—that Queen of the World, as it has been called. How many are its abject slaves, ordering their lives and measuring their tastes, not by what they think right or desirable, but by what society and the world around them dictate. Pitiable creatures! the only solid ground of happiness is not what others think of you, but what you think of yourself; not what they believe you to be, but what you know you are.

On most subjects a sensible man will be extremely tolerant. He has differed too often from himself in the course of his life to be positive with others. He also knows that opinions may differ, yet not be contradictory. Most questions have not only two sides, but many sides; they are polygonal, and, like a table of that shape, can accommodate many without elbowing. The value of anybody's opinion on any subject is much less than is popularly supposed. The fact, and not the opinion based on it, is alone of supreme importance. For that reason, what are called "fixed principles" and "settled convictions" are signs of mental debility or indolence. I think it is Ruskin who says that he would be ashamed of himself if he entertained the same opinions on any subject which he did twenty years ago. It would be a sign of ossification of the intelligence.

The characteristic of true individuality is a readiness to adopt the views of others on proper evidence, and not obstinacy, as many think. A certain flexibility of opinion strengthens personality; as the free swaying to and fro of the branches of a tree toughens the fibres of its trunk.

Obstinate asseveration is usually a sign of ignorance or falsehood. The man who swears he is telling you the truth is generally lying. When you see men in violent discussion about subjects of which they cannot know much, such as religion or politics, take a seat and laugh. They are the fools in the Comedy of Life, and the spectacle is humorous.

It is proverbial that argument never convinces, but leaves each side more strongly confirmed in its opinions. Not thus do the shrewd makers of converts go about their work. They well know that the timely hint, the insidious suggestion, the light touch, leaves the permanent impression; like the brands of animals, which to be lasting must scorch only the superficial layers of the skin, and if burnt deeper, are obliterated by the healing of the wound.

That form of opinion which is called Advice has much to do with our felicity. If a man fails, the usual explanation is that he refused to take advice. Advice which is the expression of the general results of human action—such as is supplied in such abundance in this volume—is worthy of consideration; but that which is offered to meet particular cases is generally worth about what it costs to give,—nothing. Advice is never as wise as it seems. Usually it is claimed to be the fruit of experience; but we may know the world ever so well to-day, and to-morrow our knowledge will be out of date. Good advice usually loses good opportunity. Even if by rejecting it we fail, the loss may not be real. Sometimes the money we lose turns out to be that which was best invested.

One of the choicest fruits of the culture of individuality is Decision of Character. Nothing more constantly contributes to the happiness of life. This has been so well shown by John Foster in his essay on the subject that I shall do better by the reader to persuade him to peruse it, than to enlarge on the subject here. The state of indecision, vacillation, and uncertainty, in which many persons pass a good share of their waking hours, is reason enough for the unhappiness of which they complain. The habit of decision can be readily acquired by making it a rule to decide promptly on small matters, and not allowing them again to occupy the attention.

I do not esteem highly the spirit of that Arab proverb which says,—"What you wish to conceal from your enemy, tell not to your friend;" but there is a certain reserve which every person of strong character instinctively observes toward even his intimates. It is not secretiveness, and still less taciturnity or dissimulation. Rather it is the sense of the sacredness of personality, and is the nucleus of that lofty sense of Self-reverence, which is the worthiest feeling one can entertain toward himself. There are certain recesses of the soul, certain feelings, which belong imperiously to the Ego, such as are so powerfully limned in Charlotte Bronte's poem beginning—

"When thou sleepest lulled in night,

Art thou lost in vacancy?"

which cannot be disclosed to others, though they may be divined by them.

Such reticence in no wise interferes with Sincerity of character. This is beyond all else the trait of the person of marked individuality. He alone can be sincere; not that other, who borrows his opinions from those around him, and is a mere dealer in other men's goods, and hence has none of his own to offer as security for what he says.

The casuists love to argue that veracity is a relative quality; that half a lie often conveys a more correct impression than the whole truth; that to show the seamy as well as the shiny side of great characters is an injury to the community; that courtesy obliges us to chicane with facts; that limping morality itself is much assisted by the friendly hand of mendacity. These questions may be left to the conscience of each to work out for himself; but about one kind of veracity there should be no quibbling, and that is, veracity to oneself. Deceive others if you will; but never try to persuade yourself that you are what you are not, or have what you have not. How can you expect to succeed in making yourself happy, if you studiously attempt to remain ignorant of the nature, capacities, and qualities which you aim to please?

Finally, the foundation of Individuality must be broad, if the edifice is to be solid. One must constantly have in view the symmetrical development of all the powers and faculties. He must seek many-sidedness in his knowledge and in his sympathies. All the facettes of his nature must be polished through use. Narrow views, petty interests, routine, paucity of affections, these must be avoided would he so develop his nature as to derive from it the utmost enjoyment in life.

The mission of the species is the perfecting of the individual.

For all our power in the present, we are indebted to the past; for future power—or weakness,—we shall owe the present.

The man of strong personality is not apt to perceive how much he differs from others, because he is quick to recognize the personality in them. This trait always impressed me in Walt Whitman. He seemed to take for granted that everybody had as much personality as himself. They had,—to him.

To Walt Whitman, Self was sacred,—and little else. He was intoxicated with individuality.

Distrust the current estimates of great men. They alone are not tried by their peers.

If you climb a height, you will be easier seen, but will look smaller.

It is difficult to say which is the weaker: He who cultivates self-admiration, or he whose chief aim is to elicit the admiration of others. When Cromwell entered London as Lord Protector, a flatterer called his attention to the crowds assembled to welcome him. "They would come just the same to see me hanged," was his reply.

Self-complacency is a successful counterfeit of happiness. Were it the genuine article, then the madman who believes himself Deity is the happiest of mortals. But if he is cured?

Singularity is not an effort to be oneself, but to be what others are not.

Some people cannot be blamed for affectation, for they have nothing of their own to show.

Some men, by pretending to be other than what they believe they are, show themselves in their true character.

Common minds like commonplaces. When the audience applauds, you have probably said nothing worth hearing.

It requires more courage to differ from public opinion in matters of thought than in action.

A man is apt to attribute his failure to having accepted advice; his friends, to his having rejected it.

Those listen most respectfully to advice who have resolved not to take it.

We are apt to discover the best reasons for our actions after committing them.

Most men do not base their opinions on reasoning; but their reasoning on their opinions.

Never revolt against the laws you make for yourself.

Our worst disappointments are when we disappoint ourselves. This is the feeling of Chagrin, the painful, inward acknowledgment that we "have made fools of ourselves." Few reflections are more bitter, or less easily escaped.

Our wisest warnings are often most applicable to ourselves. Steele, deviled by duns, wrote of the disgrace of contracting debts which one cannot pay; and Bacon scribbled wise saws about domestic economy at one end of the room, while his steward was robbing him at the other.

Individuality is anarchic and subversive; it accepts no institution because it is old and reverend; it brings a jewel which fits into no ready-made setting;

it cries with Walt Whitman:—

My call is the call of battle; I nourish active rebellion,

He going with me must go well-armed.

Individuality is the antithesis of egotism. He who is most himself best appreciates and most respects the self of others.

Self-distrust is nowhere more appropriate than in discussing difficult questions, and nowhere less displayed.

That we have not the ability to do, rather than that we have not the opportunity to enjoy, is the source of most of our unhappiness.

The misanthropy of the young is dissatisfaction with self; that of the old is detestation of others. Youth hopes to find life a romance, himself as its hero; age would like it a history which posterity would prize. When disappointed, youth is despairing; age is resentful.

PART IV.

How far our Happiness depends on Others.

I. What Others Give Us: Safety, Liberty, Education.

A student of human affairs has observed that it is very difficult to find happiness within oneself, and impossible to discover it elsewhere. Were the witticism reversed it would be equally true. "Imperfect happiness," observes the philosopher Kant, "arises from man's *unsocial* passions." Man's only enemy is man, but he is also his only ally. In the pursuit of happiness each must aid himself with all his might, but all his might will prove of no avail without the aid of others.

The well-being of the individual depends directly on the social organization around him. From it alone can he obtain safety, freedom, and the means of knowledge; in return, it demands respect for its rules,—that which we call Morality.

For security, safety, man is absolutely dependent on his fellows, on society. Deprived of it, a prey to well-grounded fears, he can neither develop his own powers nor enjoy the fruit of his labors. If you know the bloodhounds are on your track, the most beautiful landscape will lose its attractions. When the courtier Damocles praised Dionysius to his face as the happiest man on earth, the tyrant seated the sycophant at a luxurious repast with a sword suspended above his head by a single hair. The story is familiar to all, because its moral is a universal truth. The king stood alone on the giddy height of his power, and the dread of the inevitable fall was the vampyre that sucked the blood from all his pleasures and left them corpses before his eyes.

Men have always felt that the only security is to become members of a social organization. The savagest horde has its own, its totem, clan, or gens. But in pursuit of safety, men are apt to sacrifice freedom. To escape the fire, they plunge into the water; but neither element is their right abode. Society stands opposed to the individual. It governs by rules and averages, demands conformity, restricts liberty, dislikes personality.

Thus arises the ceaseless struggle, to and fro, over the earth, through all history, between the social and the individual theories of happiness. The constitution of the ideal civil society should realize the conditions necessary for the highest personal enjoyment. But where do we find such a constitution? Not even in theory have we reached it. On the one side are the moral tyrants, afflicted with what Mirabeau called the mania of governing, *la fureur de gouverner,* who would make men happy against their will by prescribing for them what they should eat and what they should drink, on what days they should work and on what days play. Over against them is the camp of the disclassed, unable to govern themselves, and, therefore, hating to be governed by any.

Both are equally impotent to the end both profess. Nothing but a distorted growth can result from a conformity to moral standards brought about by external compulsion. Only what a man does or leaves undone of his own free will develops and strengthens his nature. Freedom makes him a man, compulsion an animated machine. Good soldiers are not trained by fighting behind ramparts, but by exposure in the field to the enemy. What if some perish in the fray? The success of the day is cheaply bought by the fall of the few.

Limitations, restrictions, however, there must be, and that man alone is truly a freeman who recognizes and respects them. Liberty is not lawlessness; it is the ability to make the law our servant and not our master, an ability which we must acquire through our own efforts. The rights of men are equal, but they can enjoy them only so far as they qualify themselves so to do. All citizens of the United States have an equal right to pre-empt a portion of the public domain; but to secure the land they must make certain personal efforts. So it is with all other social advantages and conditions of happiness; men deserve them only so far as they cultivate a capacity for them; and not equality, but justice in their distribution, must be the final aim of every sane social compact.

The only use of this excellent government of ours, or of any other on the face of the earth, is—what? The preservation of your liberty and mine. Nothing else. Never forget this. Any government is worth paying a dollar to support, or lifting a finger to defend, only so far as it secures to each woman and man her or his greatest possible personal liberty. To the extent that it falls short of this or goes beyond it, it is worthless and an enemy. The limits of a government are plain enough, when we thus define them from the vantage-ground of individual freedom. It should protect from external enemies and internal dissensions, and from violence to person or property; it should enforce justice between man and man, and woman and man; it should extend its direct care to the weak, the immature, and the incapable; and it should supply to all the means of self-culture, of education, in its widest sense. Here its action should end. All else should be left to the individual.

There is another theory of government than this. It would treat all men as if they never come of age, or remain forever feeble-minded. It would supply them with work, take care of their pay, dictate their amusements, prohibit doubtful indulgences, and deliver from temptations by removing them. Such a government would make grown-up children, not men. It is the ideal of all priests, of most women, and of dreamers. It has at times been partially realized, and always with disastrous results to the strength of the individual character. I have seen more drunken men in one week in the State of Maine, where the sale of intoxicants is prohibited, than during three months in Italy, where their sale is unrestricted.

The advocates of all such attacks on personal liberty—be they priests or social dreamers—are not less opposed to free thought than to free action. The defense of their opinions, not the discovery of truth, is to them the purpose of research. The logical ultimatum of the one is the stake, of the other the dynamite bomb. Both would restrict the untrammeled and unbiased pursuit of knowledge.

Knowledge, however, is the twin brother of liberty and the provider for the treasury of happiness. Much more than a fine phrase is the poet's line, that "He is a freeman, whom the truth makes free." Not what he is, or what he has, but what he *knows*, gives the individual real power, and, through power, freedom and the ability to use it for the gratification of his desires through the unrestricted employment of his faculties.

The materials of knowledge are represented by the degree of civilization possessed by a nation. Their distribution should be through education—unbiased, secular, universal—co-extensive with the demand of the governed, equal to both sexes. This is within the plain province of government. Children cannot educate themselves, and ignorant parents see no need of learning. Yet the period of childhood is the golden age for instruction. It is the epoch of permanent impressions, dear and indelible, like the initials of a loved one cut on the bark of a young beech, remaining legible even when the solid heart of the aged tree is decayed.

Inertia denies the possibility of improvement. Obscurantism dislikes it. Let them pass on. Whatever a man is, there is the power for better within him; we know not how much better. Faculties trained turn from bad to good. What is a weed in the fields becomes a flower in the garden. The State cannot afford to leave education to the people. Grass grows of itself, but grain needs tillage.

How strongly this is shown in the lamentable education of women in all civilized countries! Sedulously confined to empty accomplishments and conventional moralities, they are everywhere found to be the chief supporters of decaying dogmas, serfs to social opinion, frittering away their lives in vanities which men have left centuries behind them. Both sexes are to blame for this. Men love to rule, and they fear the increased knowledge which freedom would bring to women; and women are jealous of the eminence which learning gives a sister and seek to belittle its value.

What if I refer again and again to this subject? I have too often witnessed the exceeding unhappiness of women in all grades of society not to have it frequently in my thoughts. They are more unhappy than men, as I have said before, and I believe it is mainly because they are worse educated. I know the instruction in the best schools for girls in the United States, and to what is it directed? To two ends, to be "good," and to shine in society. What they should be taught is to understand the hygiene of their own bodies, to take care of their own money, to govern their decisions by justice and reason and not by impulse, to occupy their thoughts with facts and not with fiction, and, more than all, to be independent in thought and deed, and not to allow either society or sentimentality to cast the final vote in the direction of their actions.

Such doctrine may sound heretical; so I hasten to bring to its support a reputable endorser in the person of a clergyman of the Church of England, that writer who so charmingly combines the best of humor with the best of sense, the Rev. Sydney Smith. I take it from his essay on "Female Education," an essay that ought to be read and pondered by every woman in the land, the whole burden and spirit of which is expressed in the following most pregnant sentence,—"The happiness of woman will be increased in proportion as education gives to her the habit and the means of *drawing her resources from herself.*"

How much better this than the following insufferable twaddle of Thomas de Quincey: "It is more in harmony with the retiring graces of their sexual character that they should practice a general rule of submission to the traditional belief of their own separate Church, even when that belief has long been notoriously challenged as erroneous"? He is in earnest, too; and the late Poet Laureate in "In Memoriam" said nearly the same. Blind leaders of the blind! who think that falsehood and ignorance are going to point the way to light and truth.

The fact is, the moral side of woman has been educated, and thus educated, out of all proportion to her other faculties. What is not "very stuff of the conscience" makes little or no impression on her. The Good, the Fit, the Conventional are for her the True; which is a grievous error, and retards her real progress.

Education is not only the foundation for happiness; it should and it can be made a pleasure in itself. This will sound strange to those who are principally familiar with such institutions of education as those of the Mr. Squeers or Dr. Blimber type. But the schoolmaster has himself been to school, and after flogging children for several thousand years, and thereby developing a healthy hatred of books which it is a wonder did not hurl the race back into barbarism, he has learned from Froebel and Pestalozzi and others that it is actually possible for a sane mind to study with pleasure if the chance is offered. Indeed, a learned writer who has many admirers in this country, Mr. Herbert Spencer, is able to say,—"The usual test of political legislation—its tendency to promote happiness—is beginning to be the test of legislation for the school and the nursery;" and elsewhere,—"As a final test by which to judge any plan of culture should come the question,—Does it create a pleasurable sensation in the pupil?"

This is good counsel; but, like many good things, it is also old. Two thousand years ago or so Plato wrote,—"In education, direct boys to what amuses their minds."

Security, liberty, and the means of knowledge,—these, therefore, are the conditions of happiness which every government should, and all in some measure do, offer the individual. For them, he is entirely dependent on others. In whatever delusion to the contrary his ignorance or his arrogance may plunge him, he can obtain these inestimable benefits in no other way than through the social organization, and he cannot therefore escape his liability for them. If he denies it or refuses it, the consequences will be as inevitable as they will be disastrous. He who wisely consults the conditions which determine his own happiness will not seek in isolation or self-sufficiency these elements, which can alone be obtained through the co-operation of his fellow-man.

Social progress is advanced far more by strengthening the weak than by chastising the wicked.

The sense of safety implies not merely absence of fear, but also freedom of action.

Justice should be the motto of the State; prudence that of the individual.

Self-recognition is a part of happiness; but the recognition by others of what we pride ourselves upon, is another and a large part of it.

Man is a social being; but the true aim of his social activity is to learn how to be solitary.

He who thinks it necessary to seek solitude for self-improvement often finds there is still one too many persons present.

The purpose of law is liberty; of obedience, independence; of submission, emancipation.

The well-being of the individual, not of the class, should be the aim of government. It should not be "by the people for the people," but by the people for the person.

The true moral education is that which makes every intellectual question a matter of conscience, and every matter of conscience an intellectual question.

An explanation which demonstrates the impossibility of knowing is about as satisfactory as one which imparts the knowledge desired. But there are some who call everything incomprehensible which they do not comprehend.

Many children and nearly all girls are educated by equivocations and taught truths by means of falsehoods. What have the teachers to expect when their pupils discover this fact?

There are a good many branches of education about which it is sufficient for most to know that they exist.

That moral strength is alone real which has been acquired by repeated exposure to temptation and repeated successful resistance.

We never fully acknowledge to ourselves how very human we are. We each secretly think that there is something in us not shared by any other man or woman.

Women love too deeply to be able to judge justly.

II. What we Owe Others: Morality, Duty, Benevolence.

The much-maligned Epicurus is reported to have delivered the oracular utterance,—"The man who is not virtuous can never be happy;" and poets and moralists have exhausted their ingenuity in devising variants of the well-worn line,—"'Tis virtue only makes our bliss below."

Who would have supposed that philosophers should have been found—aye, and they of high degree—who toss overboard these venerable maxims as antiquated rubbish? Yet such is the surprising case.

The mighty Kant, tearing away the cobwebs of the dogmatic philosophy, feared not to declare,—"There is not in the moral law the slightest ground for a necessary connection between Morality and Happiness;" and again,—"The goal of a perfect harmony of Desire and Duty cannot be obtained;" while in our own day the critical Alexander Bain calmly observes,—"Happiness and Virtue are independent aims and not identical. The treatment of Happiness should be dissevered from that of Ethics."

Scarcely could the contrast of the new and the old schools of thought be more vividly displayed than in these brief quotations. There are some, indeed, who have even gone farther, and maintained that the pursuit of happiness and that of virtue are not only independent, but even incompatible aims; because, writes Dr. Despine, a French psychologist of repute,—"Happiness is the satisfaction of desire, while virtue consists in doing good, not to satisfy the desire of doing it, but out of a sense of duty, and in opposition to desire." This statement, however, overlooks the existence of a moral sense and the normal pleasure derived from its gratification.

Morality and the moral sense are not to be confounded. All men have a love for the beautiful, but nowise agree as to what is beautiful; and there is just as wide and just as impassable a gulf between the various conceptions of morals, although, in all, the moral sense is present.

Morality is nothing more than the conformity of the individual to the type of the society in which he lives. It is the recognition of the debt which he owes it for securing him the privileges of safety, liberty, and education, as I have explained in the last chapter. Not his own moral sense, but the society in which he is, lays down the terms on which that debt is to be paid; and while he feels on the one side entitled to these rights, he acknowledges, on the other, his liability for his social duties in exchange for them.

There is, therefore, no such thing as a universal or even a general code of morality, nor can there be. There is no act which may not sometimes be right and sometimes be wrong. I have heard of a French writer, who composed a work entitled "The Seven Cardinal Sins," showing how under certain circumstances every one of them could be committed by a perfectly virtuous person. I have never read his book, but I delight in his doctrine. Take the Decalogue itself, written, as we are told, by the very finger of Divinity, and there is not a command in it that both Christian and Jew do not break most virtuously whenever occasion calls. "Thou shalt not kill;" and all nations spend more annually in preparations for killing by land and sea than they do in a generation for institutions of learning. "Thou shalt not rob;" and Abraham Lincoln with one glorious stroke of his pen robbed the citizens of the United States of a hundred million dollars' worth of valuable slaves. Truth-telling? The observation of Socrates in the Symposium still holds good,—"In speaking of holy things or persons, there is a general understanding that you should praise them, not that you should tell the truth about them;" witness the discussions that come up from time to time on the characters of "the Fathers of the Republic" or the books of the Bible.

In every code of morals there is one law for our friends and another for the rest of the world; our duty to our family is ever in conflict with our duty to our neighbor; and our duty to our country is opposed to our duty to humanity at large. A father who would treat other children as his own would be deemed unnatural, and a statesman who consulted the advantages of other nations would be cast out as a traitor. This is the "dualism of morals," and its necessary existence destroys all possibility of a universal and inflexible code of morals. The antagonism is not likely to decrease. The most violent contradictions between the various views of life will be likely to be found precisely in the highest culture; because there the individual comes most to his own, and is least willing to sacrifice his own rights to a society whose claims he disallows.

Men now question the right of society to demand what it does from them in exchange for the benefits it confers upon them; and they are right. Society itself must be brought to the test of the Moral Sense. This faculty is that which we also call the sense of Duty, or of "the Ought," or Conscience. It is a judge, not a lawgiver, and it derives its right of sitting in judgment from its ancient descent, dating back to the time when man first gathered together in hordes or clans under some sheltering rock for mutual aid. It is as much a part of human nature as is the love of association, and as such its satisfaction is as essential to happiness, but is by no means the whole of happiness, as so many have taught. In fact, it is often enough entirely absent, as in genuine criminals. It is now well known that these neither experience remorse for crime nor take pleasure in well-doing, whatever sentimentalists may say to the contrary.

The pleasure of the moral sense comes solely from the satisfaction of itself, and not necessarily, in the least, from the practice of virtue or benevolence or charity. The inquisitor, Torquemada, lighting the hellfires of the Inquisition, the anarchist hurling his bomb into the crowd, Judith yielding her maiden chastity to the embrace of Holofernes, all enjoyed the highest pleasure of the moral sense, because all acted in the complete conviction that they were doing right.

The man is moral who believes he is so, and the woman is chaste who considers herself such, no matter what their actions are. What we think the most fiendish crimes have been perpetrated by fervent Christians, and there are religions now numbering millions of intelligent adherents in which the prostitution of girls is considered a meritorious act.

When Adam Smith laid down the three requisites for individual happiness as health, freedom from debt, and a clear conscience, he framed a sensible prescription; but should have explained that a clear conscience in nearly all cases means simply conformity to the standard of our age and nation, not at all to any higher or abstract ideal. So far from the devotion to a lofty or unusual virtue bringing happiness, it always entails proscription, pain, and sorrow on him who advocates it. The crowd ever cry out, "Crucify him! Crucify him!" Every one of the noble army of leaders in ethical progress was in his own day branded as an infidel, cursed by the Churches, and driven forth from the enjoyments which a less developed moral sense would have permitted him to indulge. He who rises above the law is ever against the law.

Hence it is that with perfect truth, though with a lurking satire on the commonplaces of moral doctrine, Professor Bain writes,—"To realize the greatest happiness from virtue we should be careful to conform to the standard of the time and place, neither rising above nor falling beneath it; we should make our virtues apparent and showy, and perform them with the least sacrifice to ourselves; we should hold our associations with duty, as well as our natural sympathies with our fellows, only at a moderate strength."

In certain natures the satisfaction of the moral sense yields a happiness worth all sacrifices, just as in others the feeling of unrestrained liberty will be gratified at the expense of everything that the majority hold dear. Both are exceptional, and there are quite as many who suffer nothing from a violation of the sense of duty or from the loss of liberty.

No platitude is more erroneous than this,—"To be vicious is to be miserable;" for were it so, we should not have the hordes of the vicious infesting society. Far more correct is the observation of that acute observer of life, Vauvenargues, that virtue cannot make the vicious happy, *La vertu ne peut faire le bonheur des méchants.* He might have added that virtue can never make the virtuous happy, for the really virtuous man is always above the standard of his time, and is sure to suffer in consequence from the antagonism he develops, and from his sorrowful appreciation of the sentiment that prompts it.

The education of the moral sense has hitherto been retarded by two popular but mistaken doctrines; the one that the moral life is "the chief end of man;" the other that it means obedience to a code of laws.

Again I repeat that the chief end of man is the symmetrical development of all his powers and faculties and the enjoyment which he will derive from their activity, and not at all the exclusive or preponderant attention to one or the other element of his nature. His moral sense is merely the guide of the duties he owes to others, duties indispensable to his own life and liberty, but by no means exhaustive of his nature; rather, merely giving him the opportunity for the higher aim of developing himself. The moral life is but a means to an end, and not an end in itself.

The confusion of the moral life with obedience to a moral code dates back beyond history, and is almost as active to-day as ever, in spite of the efforts of such teachers as Buddha and Christ to show the falsity of it. Both proclaimed the absolute independence of the moral sense from moral laws. Such laws are either religious, expressing supposed duties to God, as the Jews believe that He forbade them to eat pork, or, as they and the Christians, that He decided that one day in seven is more sacred than the others; or they are conventional or civil, which are merely the customs, *mores*, of the nation or community.

Independent of all these codes, which for the most part are survivals, and in the present day absurd, are the Benevolent Emotions, the gratification of which to the properly developed individual constitutes a large element of personal happiness. They arise not from a sense of duty, because they do not have reference to what is due the social compact, but from sympathy, acquired or inherited. The relief of the pain of others, the administration of efficient consolation, the diminution of the sorrows of those around us, yield to ourselves a pleasurable satisfaction, a sense of appropriate activity, which is so real that it is a wonder it is not more diligently cultivated. Too many, perhaps, look for a part of their return in the gratitude of those assisted, instead of in the pleasure of the act itself, and, being disappointed, find the field of charity less flowery than they anticipated. They commit the common error of placing the end of enjoyment external to themselves instead of the means only.

The only sure method to distinguish good from evil is first to learn to discriminate true from false.

A sincere lover of truth is never wholly in the wrong; chiefly because he never claims to be wholly in the right.

The finest thought I found in Chamfort's writings—and it is wonderfully fine, deserving to be the motto of every work on the Art of Happiness—is this,—*Le plaisir peut s'appuyer sur l'illusion, mais le bonheur repose sur la vérité,* "Errors may yield us Pleasure, but truth alone can give Happiness."

Only through fulfilling his duties to society can man secure from society that which is essential to his own welfare. This is why the inward realization of the moral law becomes a part of the Art of Happiness.

A moral act is simply one which, at the time and under the special circumstances, is useful to the society in which it takes place. Hence it has nothing to do with individual Motive, which is the only Mentor recognized by the educated moral sense.

The ancient Greeks believed that the laws of human society are laws of nature, and therefore absolute. In Sophocles' tragedy, it is no excuse for Œdipus, when he kills his father and marries his mother, that he does so in absolute ignorance of the relationship. His remorse and punishment are not abated.

One school of modern writers maintains that all virtues are but vices disguised; another, that all vices are but virtues misdirected. As these terms are entirely relative, both schools are right,—and wrong.

So long as war is possible, a perfected social life is impossible; but when Justice will not be listened to in any lower notes, she must speak through the mouths of cannons.

Peace, not happiness, is the reward of virtue.

The man who professes duty as the sole guide of his life is either hypocritical or ignorant.

Weaklings and hypocrites like to extol the goodness of men; the former to allay their own fears, the latter because it reflects flatteringly on themselves.

It is no proof that a sentiment is noble because men are willing to die for it. More men knowingly sacrifice themselves to pleasure than to duty.

The lines of morality, observed Burke, differ from those of geometry; they have breadth as well as length, and for that reason will not form set and angular figures.

III. The Practice of Business and the Enjoyment of Society.

Let us grant that the true aim of the individual is his own highest development: he can reach it only through the ministry of his fellow beings. Vain the effort to seek expansion or happiness apart from his kind. The soul rusts in solitude; to be bright and keen it requires friction with others.

Alone, it starves and pines, grows misshapen and distorted; in company, it gives and receives, assists others, and is in turn assisted. Let us do no injustice to the balm and the blessings of solitude; but the growth of the world is due to the blending and the striving of mind with mind.

The word which expresses this is Association. It conveys various degrees of intimacy, from the lowest, that of the ordinary intercourse of Business and Society, through the increasingly closer ties of Fellowship, Comradeship, and Friendship, up to that dearest of all, wherein the two sexes unite to cast the rays of life into the infinite future, Love and Marriage.

There is nothing in any of these that demands the sacrifice of the individual. The gauge which marks the high-water line in them all is one and the same—the maintenance of the utmost freedom of the individual along with the utmost sympathy and accordance with the individuality of others. As it is only through these, through participation in all of these relations of association, that the highest degree of personal happiness can be attained, I shall consider each in turn very briefly, little more than hinting of those maxims and principles which stand approved as contributing to a reasonable success and a wise enjoyment of them.

Dealing with men is the daily business of life; but a knowledge of human nature, even in this restricted relation, is the latest knowledge which one acquires.

The first maxim is *to distrust*.

"All men are liars," said the Psalmist; and there is no stronger proof of the saying than that all men deny it. History and sermons and sympathy combine to conceal or to modify the truth, in order that we may walk in peace with our fellow-men. Be it so. But at least, in our own minds, let us acknowledge facts. We are none the better ourselves for believing others to be better than they are. "The transacting of business," observes Bacon, "is chiefly a commerce with fools;" my comment upon which is, that he will be the worst fooled who thinks he is the only wise man; of which my Lord of

Verulam is said to have been a conspicuous example.

Insincerity has no limit. If a man does not show what he is when first you meet him, wait a year to decide. The insincere aim most to deceive by what most they show. Concerning them, therefore, follow the Italian maxim, believe the incredible and doubt the probable. The very pious cashier, not the thoughtless clerk, will be the one to run away with the money.

The second maxim is *to trust.*

Confidence in others is the corner-stone both of fortune and felicity. It is the grateful dew which fertilizes the flowers of sincerity, of truthfulness, and honor; and even common honesty will wither if exposed to the scalding breath of suspicion. Reputation lives in the minds of others, and if we know ours has no fixed abode there, but is harbored as a doubtful and distrusted intruder, our staunchest argument for preserving it is gone.

He who can happily combine the oil and vinegar of these two maxims in his dealings with men, will carry with him a charm which will guard him from the bitterest disappointments to which we are liable in the hard contest for material aims.

Business intercourse we cannot avoid; but we seek it for other ends than pleasure; social intercourse is that which we pursue for enjoyment only,—or, at least, pretend to. Hence, we call it specifically "Society;" and we distinguish it into certain fanciful grades, as "good society," "the best society," and "high life." Men and women enter it equally, and the spirit of it is held to be apart from, even quite the reverse of, that of business life. Many men and all women look upon it as the field in which the chief victories of their careers must be won and the main elements of their happiness discovered.

Why sneer at such sentiments? The drawing-room, the only stage on which the two sexes meet on equal terms, is the innermost sanctuary of civilization, and the hostess is high priestess of the shrine. Its development registers the epochs in the history of culture. Francis I has two special claims on the praise of posterity; the one, that he proclaimed himself honored by the friendship of Titian; the other, that he was the first to admit women to the court society of France. The drawing-room confers the last degree in the liberal arts. No education is complete which has not received its finishing touches at the hands of a refined woman; and enlightenment will first deserve its name when her rights are everywhere as much respected and her influence as freely acknowledged as they are now in her own parlors.

Good-will is the basis of good society. He who quits a company, pleased, and conscious of having pleased, is its model member. There is nothing derogatory in this. Conceal it as we may, the secret motive of our every effort is the hope of pleasing somebody else. The interchange of kindly courtesies and approving expressions is a commendable pastime. He who prides himself on being "beholden to nobody" is a pseudo-philosopher. The true philosopher enjoys society, but is not dependent on it for his enjoyment.

Would-be superior men have inveighed against society because its members are and must be for the most part "ordinary people," and its topics common-place. Really superior men prefer ordinary people, because, as Goethe so well said, "They are more human." Nobody was common-place to the eye of that great master, because each represented the species. It is certainly true that in the long run, and for "human nature's daily use," ordinary people are the most agreeable. We really should not desire high thinking in high life. People fraternize more readily on lower levels because they are broader. Nations gather together on plains, not on mountain tops. These are suitable for star-gazers and eagle-hunters.

Those who dislike society are usually those who are not at ease in it, from lack of early training. Few enjoy dancing who have learned from an awkward master, and a lifetime is not long enough to comb the hayseed from a farmer boy's hair.

The one maxim for success in society is to be agreeable; and the agreeable man is he who agrees with others. Society expects persons to offer enjoyment and pleasure, not improvement. One should accept men as they are and not seek to change them; it is a less task to adapt yourself to others than them to you. One that enters a company that he likes, is liked by it; but nothing is so justly exasperating as a show of superiority.

The aim of society is to bring about a closer union of its members by having them meet on planes of thought and emotion which are common to all. The expression of discordant ideas and feelings, be they higher or lower, is, therefore, out of place. On the other hand, a company is harmonized, and its elements happily fused together, by some general impression made on all at the same moment, and the enjoyment of all is correspondingly heightened. This may be by a strain of music appropriately introduced, by a few apt remarks on a topic of general interest, or by the exhibition of curious or beautiful objects. The sense of a sentiment in common is at once established, and the company feels that each knows the other better for this property in commonalty. The skillful hostess knows how often and by what devices thus to promote the unity of her guests. Multiply the ties which bind society together and you multiply the pleasure it yields and the benefits which are derived from it.

Really good society is not selfish, nor does it encourage selfishness. Rather it is based on a certain sacrifice of self. Those circles offer little enjoyment where each aims at nothing but his own; amusement is absent where no one endeavors to amuse others. Nor is it unjustly censorious. Its judgments are generally recognized as fair, and nothing so fortifies the moral sense as the approval of the society in which one is accustomed to move; while the terrors of the Hereafter are small compared to its disapproval. The stoutest minds have acknowledged this. "Who can see worse days," asks Bacon, "than he who yet living doth follow at the funeral of his own reputation? I can desire no greater place than in the front of good opinion."

It is quite true that this power, like that of all irresponsible autocrats, is sometimes abused to the injury of the worthy; but the harm is slight compared to the results which are good. True, also, that general society is a poor test of a man's real nature. One may possess many agreeable qualities and yet fail to be agreeable, through lack of good taste or early training in their use under social conditions. Or, again, though a kindly disposition makes a man popular, it by no means follows because a man is popular that he has a kindly disposition. We must accept society with these deficiencies, for in spite of them all it is a potent auxiliary in the pursuit of happiness.

Genuine kindliness of heart,—this is the sweetest trait of human nature. Unfortunately, it is one of the rarest; so that society, which appreciates it so highly that it cannot exist without at least its semblance, substitutes for it—Politeness.

Though a semblance only, it is a noble counterfeit. Urbanity presages perfected Humanity. It is the outward and visible sign of what should be the inward and spiritual nature. It is a prophecy of the Golden Age and is based on the Golden Rule. When some one asked Aristotle how we should conduct ourselves toward our associates, he replied,—"We should treat them as we wish them to treat us."

Politeness is the only currency which costs nothing and buys much. Its tenders are counters and yet pass as coin. Who but a fool, therefore, would refuse to use them liberally? Such fools there are, however, and in abundance. It is a key which has the pleasant power of both closing the doors below and opening those above us; for there is no bar to the unwelcome familiarity of inferiors equal to scrupulous politeness, and no passport so sure to the esteem of our superiors in age or station.

Cheap as it is, it is too precious to be wasted, and like the free gifts of nature, water or sunlight, there are occasions when it must be doled out in small quantities, and at all times be dispensed with a provident hand. Few social blunders are more painful than to display a warmth of manner which is not reciprocated; and there are rude natures who cannot distinguish kindliness of behavior from weakness of purpose.

The common lien of society is Talk; and the talk must be essentially small talk. No greater blunder could be committed than to suppose that society wants, or ought to want, Conversation, in the dignified sense of that term, in which an idea is introduced and expanded, a proposition developed, or an argument stated. Nothing of the sort. "The best conversation," observes Mr. Malloch, "is never worth remembering." Perhaps he had in his mind the remark of Talleyrand, who said that the finest converser he ever heard was his own mother, but that he was unable to recall a single pointed or brilliant expression she had used.

Small talk is in society what small change is in the daily affairs of life,—you need it twenty times for your gold-piece once. It is no such easy matter to master the art of it. To talk much and to say little one must be very clever or a fool; and the still higher art of putting others to their best paces, so that you act only as starter in the race while others win the purse, asks an amount of tact which is equaled only by the self-denial involved.

The expert in talk will aim to please and not to instruct; he will not disturb the convictions of elderly persons who have made up their minds; nor the self-complacency of any by a display of superiority, especially in his judgment or reasoning powers; if he boasts, it will be of his luck and not of his cleverness; he may compliment a woman on her beauty, but never a rich man on his riches; he will contradict only those who disparage themselves, and if he dips into a deep question, he will only stir it and not settle it; he will avoid allusions to his own ailments, but sedulously inquire about those of others; but his chief aim will be to find out first whether the person whom he addresses prefers to talk or to listen, and scrupulously let him have his way.

When all are of one mind, what is left to say worth hearing?

Save your best thoughts for your best friends.

Frivolity is the armor of good society, worn to protect it against the violence of passions and the ennui of enthusiasms.

Subservience to society is in man what "protective mimicry" is in insects,—an unconscious tendency to imitation for the purpose of self-preservation.

Youth looks to be received in society with greater sympathy than it finds; age will find more than it generally expects.

Acquaintances rate us first at the value we put on ourselves; later at the value we prove to them.

Those who visit you, find out how you live; you must visit them to find out how they live.

Forgive if you can, but do not forget. Characters change little, and a base action is a landmark worth remembering.

A lie comes readier in society than in solitude; but for all that, it is easier to deceive oneself than others.

Only those of violent prejudices violently attack the prejudices of others.

It is a rule in polite society not to refer to three subjects—a man's false hair, his religion, or his politics; and for the same reason—because neither is his own, but merely borrowed from others.

Curious inconsistency! People talk willingly about their physical ailments, but unwillingly about their moral defects; though the former cannot be mended by discussing them, and the latter might be.

Silence is often sanatory. There are subjects, thoughts, and memories which, like certain bodily functions, cannot be avoided, but should not be talked about.

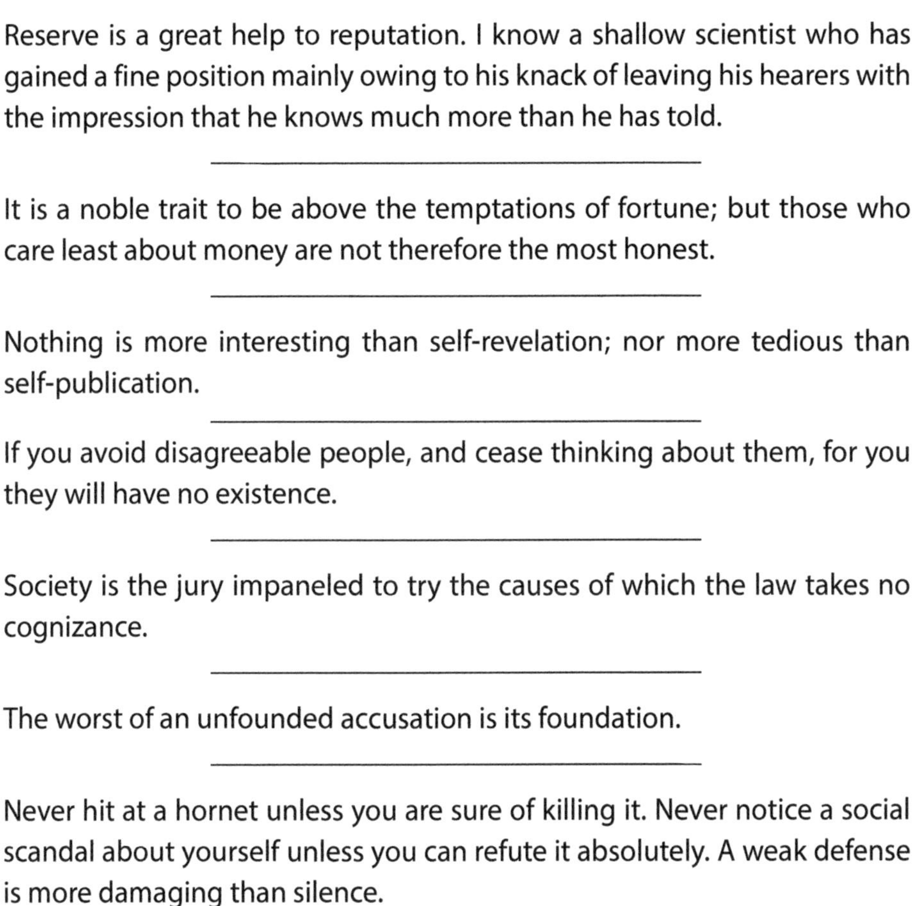

Reserve is a great help to reputation. I know a shallow scientist who has gained a fine position mainly owing to his knack of leaving his hearers with the impression that he knows much more than he has told.

It is a noble trait to be above the temptations of fortune; but those who care least about money are not therefore the most honest.

Nothing is more interesting than self-revelation; nor more tedious than self-publication.

If you avoid disagreeable people, and cease thinking about them, for you they will have no existence.

Society is the jury impaneled to try the causes of which the law takes no cognizance.

The worst of an unfounded accusation is its foundation.

Never hit at a hornet unless you are sure of killing it. Never notice a social scandal about yourself unless you can refute it absolutely. A weak defense is more damaging than silence.

It is a much admired art to turn the weaknesses of others to our own profit. How sublime would be the science which would direct their strength to their own true interests!

IV. On Fellowship, Comradeship and Friendship.

Man is slow to understand how human he is. He thinks he can measure himself by other standards than himself, but all his circuits lead him home again; his most positive knowledge is of himself, and by analogy of his own kind. With a wise recognition of the limits of his own nature he should seek happiness in the conditions of existence known to him and especially among his own species, where alone he can find beings whose endowments are the same, and whose affinities and sympathies respond to his own.

Society, as I have said, is the common field of intercourse in civilized life, and it makes for itself its own various limitations and restrictions. Other methods of Association are based on quite different principles, but have all been organized with the aim of increasing happiness, and all therefore deserve the cultivation of him who is sedulous about his own. The two motives which give them origin are, the one, Interest; the other, Sympathy. The former I may call Fellowships; the latter, Comradeships.

Fellowships, composed of those who *follow* the same business, trade, or profession, and thus have an interest in common,—this is what the word means. They are the guilds, unions, lodges, clubs, societies, associations, companies, which swarm so in our day, whose members are held together by a desire of mutual assistance in making money, or raising wages, or providing against misfortune, or maintaining privileges, or buying cheap, or paying each other's funeral expenses, or in a thousand other ways advancing the interests, and thus relieving the burdens and increasing the enjoyment, of their members. I knew a man who belonged to over three hundred such associations, and as he was in other respects a sensible person, he probably found a profit in this multiplication of ties.

It is a discovery of modern times of no mean importance that after several thousand years of open trial, government and religion and friendship and love have all failed in relieving the misery of human life, but that the intelligent recognition of the mutuality of interests does not fail; and, when properly organized, may be counted on with utmost confidence to prevent most of the disasters and to secure most of the essential material blessings of life,—far beyond the dreams of the most sanguine reformers of earlier generations. There is no reason why we should have the poor always with us, except the ignorance of men as to their own material interests or their indifference to them; and these difficulties must in time diminish, if not disappear. Through association for mutual aid in buying and selling, in labor and investment, in defense and assistance, in credit and insurance, and the like, the date is almost calculable when the deserving poor will as a class no longer exist, and extreme indigence will mean either idleness or crime.

The rock on which most such schemes have shattered has been that in their blind effort at mutuality they have overlooked the prime import of individuality—the freedom and autonomy of each member. It should never be forgotten that the only value of any scheme of association is the development of the individual. Any society which does not make this its first and clearly announced purpose is doomed to a deserved failure. There is no sentiment in such associations. They classify men like bricks or boxes, according to the externals or accidents of their professions or places. They pay no heed to personality beyond the one element in it which they are formed to take cognizance of. For that very reason they are apt to demand disproportionate sacrifices for this, and to encroach on liberty by unjust demands on the member's time, labor, leisure, or money. They are liable to reach a point where the benefits they confer are not worth the sacrifices they require. This is the history of many labor unions in the United States, and it is the characteristic of all the so-called socialistic schemes for improving society. In all of them society is looked upon as paramount to the individual, instead of the individual as paramount to society; whereas, his development is that alone for which society has any right to exist.

Comradeship differs from Fellowship as social does from business life. In it there is no question of interests in common, but only of tastes in common—a mutuality which exists often to the sad injury of interests. Comrades are birds of a feather, who assemble because they resemble—in accordance with the French proverb, *Qui se rassemblent, s'assemblent.* They all like dogs, or whist, or yachts, or music, or old books, or four-in-hands, or spectral analysis,—any of the occupations of choice which are pursued for the pleasure they yield.

In modern life this form of Association has largely taken the place of Friendship as it was understood by the ancients. It is better adapted to the bustle and scurry of these days, when the busy worker has not time to cultivate the amenities of sentiment, but desires to find others who share his favorite tastes, and a ready-made sympathy which he need not be at the trouble of looking after, but which is always at hand when he wants it. This he finds in such comradeships, where each comes because he has likings similar to the others, and is therefore sure to be a pleasant arrival. Each thus gratifies his own taste and increases its capacity for gratification; for tastes are like magnets,—the more they are used the stronger becomes their power of attraction.

The higher grades of comradeship are seen in artistic, literary, and scientific societies, which pursue their objects for the love of the subject, and not for commercial or other material ends. The intellectual communion which they yield to their members is a pleasure of a very high order, and an additional and valuable advantage which they possess is that they bring workers in the same fields of unselfish pursuits together, soften the asperities which ignorance of each other's personalities might allow to remain, and often pave the way for warm and abiding friendships. Those men of science or artists who hold themselves aloof from such reunions usually do so through self-distrust or undue sensitiveness, and sin both against their own happiness and the prosperity of their favorite employment.

Both the religious and the moral life—they are not the same—should find their chief activity in the sphere of comradeship. It was the beautiful ideal of George Fox that the Church of the future should be a Society of Friends. The ideal is too lofty for human nature; but it is quite possible and should be a daily occurrence that the members of a church or a society united for the development of the benevolent or religious sentiments should display as much mutual good feeling and as warm a personal interest in the common purpose, as, say, dog-fanciers who belong to the same kennel club.

Friendship is far rarer than Comradeship, because it is more delicate and requires a higher type of character. Most men are incapable of it, and therefore cannot distinguish it from a mere community of tastes. It goes much farther, embracing the whole nature, and lifting the relation out of the plane of interests or tastes into that of sentiment and spiritual sympathy. No one is capable of friendship who thinks what use he can make of it. Friendship is free trade, and knows neither charity, robbery, nor reciprocity. It keeps neither a debit nor a credit account, and it leaves no room for ingratitude, because the credit of each party is unlimited.

The completest friendship is that in which the utmost sympathy is united with the utmost independence. The differences must not be so great as to prevent a thorough understanding, nor so small as to do away with admiration for the personal qualities of each other, and some desire to emulate them.

These phrases do not mean that we should look for perfection in friends. Quite the contrary. What could be more fatiguing than perfection? Its monotony would be unendurable. The affection for friends is not a tribute paid to their merits. Their very faults often endear them. We do not wish them removed. For ourselves, it may be well to retain some of those defects which give our friends pleasure; though this is to be taken with reserve; for, on the other hand, a great charm in a friend is that he brings us not what we expected, but something equally pleasant which we did not expect.

Friendship is strengthened by a certain amount of reserve. Few persons, to use the slang of the studio, "strip well." Every one gains by veiling some of his parts. For the same reason we should not ask nor desire complete confidence from a friend. There are always secrets which it is better not to know. We may inquire the cause of his despondency, for sympathy and aid are natural to the sentiment of friendship; but should wait to be told the sources of his elation.

In a similar manner absence for not too long a time strengthens friendship by allowing its value to be felt, and the imagination to clothe the absent in some of the fanciful and beautiful garbs of the ideal. But too prolonged a stay leaves friendship a memory rather than a passion.

"But what!" some one will exclaim. "Are we to set about making and keeping friends with the same attention as if we were raising hot-house fruit?" Yes, precisely so; but if a friend is not in your estimation worth as much as a bunch of Hamburg grapes, I assure you it will be time wasted for you to try. When people complain that they have no friends, inquire what efforts they have made to get and keep them. True friendship is rare because it is rarely sought for. When Lord Bacon wrote, "There is little friendship in the world, and least of all between equals," the great Chancellor unwittingly testified to the truth of those charges of perfidy which posterity has brought against his name. Friends must be diligently sought for, and when found must be sedulously cherished. Dr. Johnson never said a wiser word than when he gave the advice, directed especially to those who are advancing in years, "to keep our friendships in constant repair."

Such a relation of sentiment between men can scarcely be formed in later life. As trees grow old their fibres become rigid, and their branches cannot be interlocked to arch a bower. But, by a delightful compensation of nature, it is precisely at this period of life that the sweetest friendships of all are formed—those between men and women. Some have doubted these, and I grant you most are incapable of them; but in facts and friendships there is no such thing as gender. There are too many beautiful examples in history to allow room for scepticism here.

Need I count them? Need I refer to the friendship between Chateaubriand and Madame Recamier, extending over thirty years, during which she was the guide, consoler, and confidante of the great statesman and author; not as a learned woman,—for that she was not,—but as a truly sympathetic soul? Need I quote from that charming volume of letters, the *Briefe an eine Freundin,* which testify to the long, the loving, and the pure bond that united Wilhelm von Humboldt to Charlotte Diede?

Or is there occasion to dwell on that instance which enshrines elements of sweetness even beyond these, the friendship between Michael Angelo and Vittoria Colonna? Think of the inspired and self-centred artist, living alone with his dreams of matchless beauty, meeting no man worthy of admittance even to the threshold of his affections, he who could write from Rome to his nephew in Florence, "I have no friends; I need none and wish none;" finding at last in the noble and tender soul of this distinguished woman the sentiments and sympathy for which he had been unconsciously longing, and which were necessary to complete the symmetry of both his own life and hers!

The burden laid on Beauty is, that it can have many lovers but no friends.

A very positive character is at first pleasing. We ourselves are troubled by so many problems that it is a relief to think,—"Here is one who has solved them all." But we soon find that such characters merely slam the door in the face of importunate inquiries.

Men's characters are polar forces; the stronger they repel some, the stronger they attract others.

The society of those who enjoy is alone enjoyable.

Be select in your friends, but miscellaneous in your acquaintances. Ask not sympathy from the latter nor assistance from the former.

If you would keep friends, shun explanations.

If you doubt the persistence in adversity of what is called friendship, make friends with an impecunious debtor.

Men admire women who try to please them; women admire men who, they believe, have qualities worthy of admiration.

We like those who can be useful to us, and love those to whom we can be useful.

The secret of gaining friends is to cultivate within ourselves the capacity for friendship.

New acquaintances cannot take the place of old friends; but when your teeth wear out, an artificial denture is a vast advantage over bare gums.

Be sure that the man who boasts of a hundred friends, has none.

V. Love, Marriage, and the Family Relation.

"It is not good that the man should be alone." Venerable maxim! First reflection of the Creator on the species! Standing condemnation of all schemes of celibacy, of all orders of monks and nuns, vestals and spiritual eunuchs!

The character of any man or woman who leads the single life is incomplete, lacking in fullness of sympathy for certain aspects of our common nature, not perfectly rounded to the orb of man's whole life. All examples, even the highest, give evidence of this. No man who has not had a wife whom he loved can understand what love is; he who is not a parent, can never appreciate the feelings of a father.

The fruition of life, even on the lowest terms, is impossible without the union of the sexes. The first Napoleon, in one of his letters, describing the essential needs of man, numbered them as three,—food, shelter, woman. All doctrines and social theories which conflict with this primordial law of the life of the species are unnatural, and their tendency is lowering to the progress of the race. Maternity, not virginity, is the holier state. Celibate orders have proved as sterile in intellectual as in physical offspring.

Love, marriage, children, the family,—the emotions and feelings, the affections and the ideas, which centre around these foci of human activity are essential elements in every life which is lived to the full measure of its powers. Nothing can take their places. Happiness without them is not human.

The emotion of Love belongs to those whose aims are ideal, because it is concerned with the future evolution of the species. In the iridescent glow of this master-passion its object never seems a mere human being, a man or a woman, but is invested with a charm unseen by the eye, not expressed in form or color, endowed with the power of exciting the soul to an indefinite and passionate expansion. It is the inaudible appeal of unborn posterity for its share in the world of Being.

Hence it is that Love is so powerfully excited by Beauty, by the symmetry and traits which foreshadow the final physical perfection of the race, the unconscious but unceasing struggle of organic nature toward nobler transformations, toward the building of a tabernacle fit to be a shrine for the activities of a higher life.

Though hundreds of volumes have been written in poetry and prose on the subject of Love, it remains unexhausted, because it is inexhaustible. Its seed-field is the boundless future, its message concerns all posterity. There is something in it deeper than the emotion of any single heart, farther reaching than any individual effort. There is a secret about it which can never be wholly told, which it were a profanation to try to express. Even between loving ones, it is better not to talk much of it, nor too curiously to think about it. When true and pure, it will be manifested without words in ennobling the character and elevating its aims and actions.

The attraction of woman for man is her invisible presage of motherhood. This it is which lends the nameless charm to the maiden and the sacred dignity to the matron. Around her, centre all those sentiments which constitute the Home, the family, and the parental affections. These find their proper expression in Marriage.

The history of the institution of marriage is a curious narrative. Every conceivable relation of the sexes has been established by one community or another, and sanctioned by the moral sense of the time and place. There have been hordes where the relations have been communal or miscellaneous; others, where a man had many wives; others, as in Thibet to-day, where the woman would have many husbands; sometimes the woman selects the man, at others the man the woman, and elsewhere the marriage is arranged by third parties; in some, marriage is indissoluble, in others, more or less easily annulled; while in certain religious societies in our own country the method of selective and temporary unions has been practiced. The result of all these experiments has been to show that the happiness of both parties is best consulted by strictly monogamous or pairing marriages, where each exerts a certain amount but not entire freedom of selection, and where the lien can be canceled when it proves clearly detrimental to the felicity of either.

Very few words will be necessary to defend the first of these three conditions. Under whatever form we find polygamy, whether legalized, as in Mohammedan countries, or sanctioned by religion, as among the Mormons, or winked at by usage, as in mistress-keeping, it inevitably results in the degradation of the woman and her subjection to the dominion of lower impulses. To every one who believes that her happiness demands equal attention to that of the man, all schemes of polygamy stand condemned.

The second condition I have stated will need more defense. Especially in our country is it unpopular to oppose the course of love. "Let me not," exclaims the great dramatist, "to the marriage of true minds admit impediment." Yet all will admit certain impediments. The laws of many States prohibit the marriage of near of kin, of first cousins, and of uncles with nieces, although in Germany unions of the latter class are very common.

Immature age does legally, and should always, act as a bar to marriage. At what period of life marriage is likely to prove most happy is a curious question, which has never been properly studied. The physiologist, basing his opinion on grounds of his science, would say that the woman should be between twenty and thirty, and the man between twenty-five and thirty-five. Dr. Johnson, regarding the question from another point of view, made the wise observation,—"Those who marry late are best pleased with their children, and those who marry early with their partners."

Apart from questions of immature age and near relationship, marriages in the United States are generally contracted without restriction. The young of both sexes are usually conceded full liberty to make their own selection, the burden of the support of both being generally assumed by the husband. The consequence is that such unions are frequently entered upon with slight real acquaintance of each other, the wife is wholly dependent, and the husband has a heavy load to carry,—conditions calculated to intensify the struggle for existence and diminish the happiness of home.

From considerable observation of family life in both countries, I believe that the French system is superior to ours. In a French family of the middle or upper classes, the parent who desires to marry a daughter, for instance, takes pains to introduce and recommend young men of suitable station. No coercion is used on either side. Only when an affection naturally springs up is the union decided upon. A marriage-settlement is drawn by which each of the young couple receives a certain amount of property, wholly independent of the control of the other. Thus they are freed from the severest pressure of monetary anxiety, and, what is especially valuable, the wife has a recognized place of power, and secures her rightful prestige in the family circle. I have often observed how superior is the position of the wife in France to what it is in this country. The reason is in the better method of forming marriages.

A sympathetic marriage is the happiest condition of human life; but one without sympathy is a hateful servitude. How distressing to be obliged to live *for* those whom we cannot bear to live *with*!

The number of unhappy marriages in the United States may be guessed from the records of the divorce courts, which register only some of the most unhappy. The divorces granted annually sever nearly thirty thousand couples, and this although in many States such separation is costly, slow, and difficult. These figures represent, therefore, but a small fraction of the marriages which are galling the backs of one or both of the parties concerned.

When we reflect what the true foundations of the marital relations should be,—love, affection, sympathy,—it would appear wholly foreign to its character that it should be made an obligatory fetter and a continued curse by any law, civil or religious. The moral sense, personal affection, parental feeling, and the sentiment of society, would seem to be sufficient to preserve all those unions which should be preserved. Their severance should be left to the option of the parties concerned alone. Surely the happiness of the individual would be better consulted by such an arrangement than by that which now prevails.

Marriages, so far from being entered upon with greater recklessness, would then be more cautiously undertaken, because their durability would depend on mutual satisfaction. The woman would have full equality of rights, and not be a miserable sacrifice to unjust laws, as now she often is. It would be a step toward the ideal of the marriage state, which is a union based on love, in which each party has absolutely equal rights and stands pledged to equal duties, and neither is bound to the other longer than love and duty are respected. Neither government nor religion should put obstacles in the way of the dissolution of marriage other than those safeguards of the interests involved, which attend the termination of all important contracts.

Deep thinkers on the relations of life in goodly number have long advocated these views. They have been those of John Milton, of William von Humboldt, of John Stuart Mill. Nor is there anything in them which an enlightened moral or religious sentiment should oppose; rather the contrary. As Milton so well says in his Treatise on Divorce,—"Where Love cannot be, there can be left of wedlock nothing but the empty husk of an outside matrimony, as undelightful and unpleasing to God as any other kind of hypocrisy."

The object of marriage is the Family. Love claims immortality through posterity. The hidden though ever-present purpose of the union of the sexes is the perpetuation and evolution of the species. Any union which avoids this object is destructive, and not creative of true happiness. We are told of the ancient ascetic sect of the Essenes that the sexes united in marriage, but remained chaste; and had families of children, but gathered them from among the foundlings and homeless orphans of the highways. Their impossible example does not merit the praise, as it has not enlisted the imitation of, later generations. The maternal and paternal affections, the love of family and the pleasures derived from the ties of kindred, are enjoyments which the properly constituted individual will never be willing to sacrifice unless constrained thereto by mighty and exceptional conditions. The tacit assumption of mutual aid and confidence between brothers and sisters, and the intimacy which is fostered by even remoter degrees of relationship, are beneficent elements of the social compact, and contribute largely to the happiness of the individual.

The Family, as we understand it, is distinctly a product of high civilization. In savage tribes the ties of consanguinity are quite different. In many, for instance, the father is scarcely regarded as a relation, blood kin being counted through the mother only. The rise of the paternal or patriarchial form of the family appears at a higher stage of culture; and when, as among the Etruscans and Romans, it was coincident with a recognized equality in marriage, society advanced with rapid strides.

Some believe that the theory of the family, as it has so long prevailed in Europe, is inappropriate for this country, and hence that it is disappearing among us, as unsuited to the development of our forms of culture. Children desire their liberty earlier, and parents are ready to comply with their requests. No ties other than material ones are recognized as constituting a family unit. It will be for the future to decide whether the greater personal independence thus secured has been of more value to the happiness of the race than the elements of affection sacrificed in obtaining it.

Law is the bond of the state, love, of the family. The former rules best by precept, the latter by example.

Those marriages are ominous which transmit miseries.

The family tie differs from the tie of friendship in that it binds together interests rather than sympathies.

Love, says Michael Angelo in one of his Sonnets, is the mental impression of ideal beauty:—

Amore e un concetta di bellezza

Immaginata, cui sta dentro al cuore.

The aims of the child centre around his maturity; those of the man around his posterity.

The generations unborn are the sovereigns of the world, and the goals we are running for are invisible. Posthumous aims are the potent.

The heart of every woman is like a page written with sympathetic ink. It seems blank, but warm it sufficiently, and you will find a love-letter written on it.

Cara amica, beware of that tendency in your nature to repose utter confidence. Learn that nought is so fragile as Faith. It is like those delicate vases of Venetian glass which a single drop of poison is said to shiver into atoms. Better the homely ware which will toss it out, and fill again with wine. It is a law of reasoning that full belief is disproved by a single event, but partial belief only by a series of events. But what have you to do with reasoning? you who must trust "not at all, or all in all"? and bless you for it, fated, foolish friend.

A man weeps for the lost loved one; a woman for the lost love.

Love is the language in which the gods speak to man, observes Plato. Unfortunate is he who hears it not; doubly unfortunate he who hears, but comprehends it not.

True love is love of love; not love of the pleasures of love.

  ☺

PART V.

The Consolations of Affliction.

I. The Removal of Unhappiness.

Suffer we must. No position is exempt, no foresight can avoid it. Neither the self-abnegation of asceticism nor the visions of superstition relieve from that law. The latter do but deceive and the former atrophies the soul. Far better to seek in the strength of our own minds and in the helpful sympathy of others those sources of Consolation which will enable us to bear pain and grief and disappointment, without allowing them to pass into ennui, gloom, and the distaste for life. Calm reflection, clear reasoning, and the soothing kindness of those who love us, will prepare us to meet and bear the evils of life, without having recourse to the illusions of credulity or the aridities of stoicism.

The mind can be trained to forecast the probable good and ill of its career, and thus prepare itself for even the worst of fates, without being plunged into the hopelessness of despair. We can learn to suffer, and to find even suffering good. To a trained mind, no deprivation is an absolute misfortune.

What is more, this very training is the best of preservatives as well as the best of alleviatives; for by it we are prompted and enabled to take wise measures to avoid those evils which our forethought brings to our mind.

Consolation we all need, all must have, all should give, if we would develop the sweeter and nobler elements of our natures. He who through mistaken pride or stubborn distrust refuses to seek it, does but dwarf his powers and darken his perceptions to the beauties of the world around him. To impart and to receive the solace of sympathetic words and kindly offices belong to the highest ministrations of friendship and love and charity. Those characters in history around whose faces shines brightest the aureole of glory have been those who have soothed the sorrows and bound up the wounds of the despairing sons of men.

Fortunately, if evils are many, so are the sources of consolation. We may seek them in ourselves, from others, or from a correct comprehension of the laws of nature; and when these prove inadequate, we may still win the victory, by discovering that Sorrow itself is not an enemy but a friend, a veiled and ghostly guide, who leads us, as the spirit of Virgil led Dante, and as only Sorrow can lead, through the realms of gloom and woe to undreamed-of fields of serenity and light.

Only in hint and outline shall I sketch this part of my plan. It is too vast to attempt more. Some of the reflections which in the sadder hours of my own life I have found of avail I shall present in detached fragments; for the spirit in the shadow needs but a single ray to illume its path. The moods of sorrow are many, and one suggestion may soothe where a score of others find no application. What I offer are suggestions only, to be expanded by the reader as he finds one or another of them suitable to his own case.

Two very consoling reflections are: First, how much of the unhappiness of life springs from preventable causes, and next, how little of it arises from actual evils. When we deliberately investigate, catalogue, and analyze what we ourselves and our neighbors are distressed about, we are inclined to say that the chief aim of human effort is not happiness, but rather that each shall make himself as unhappy as possible.

Look at the list! Desires and aims which are plainly inconsistent and contradictory with each other; hopes which reason clearly shows are doomed to disappointment, because they are unfounded or exaggerated; anxieties which are visibly causeless or useless; mistaken estimates of our own powers, which honest reflection would correct; envy of the supposed better fortune of others, when often they are more unhappy than ourselves; fears for a future which we may never reach; regret for a past which we can never recall; open-eyed abuse or neglect of opportunities; indulgence in passions or appetites which we know to be harmful; needless risk or sacrifice of health or liberty or money.

Think of how much of your unhappiness has arisen from one or other of these causes, and then take comfort in the thought how much it lies in your power to be far happier than you are.

There is an advantage in the multiplicity of miseries. One deep vexation is often more fatal to happiness than several. It becomes a fixed idea, monopolizes the mind, and is more dangerous to its health, than when one is obliged "to take up arms against a sea of troubles." Regret not, therefore, when clouds darken all the horizon; better this, than the single sky-specter, in whose bosom is the whirlwind, and on whose path follows destruction.

When little matters annoy you, remember that it is a proof that your condition is a peculiarly happy one. Great sorrows leave no room for slight irritations. The man on the rack does not feel the prick of a pin.

Tears are the medicinal waters provided by nature for healing the sickened spirit. They are the stream which by its overflowing renews the fertility of the wastes left arid by woe. But, like these greater streams, their excess brings devastation.

Unhappiness is sometimes only a bad habit. Weeping eyes are quick to tears, and grief is a guest that stays on slight urging.

Ill-fortune and plenty of it is the very stimulus some natures need to bring out the best that is in them. There is a dead weight about them, and bad luck is the only lever that will lift it. Without its prod, they would sink into lethargy and become like Chaucer's

> "Eclympasteyre,
>
> That was the God of Slep' is heire,
>
> That slepte, and did none other worke."

There are two inconsistencies of grief which surpass all others: the one, when it leads us to regret that which we might have enjoyed, long after the time when we could have enjoyed it is past; the other, when it makes us the sadder to-day, because we enjoyed ourselves yesterday.

There is something humorous in the two most popular methods of consolation. The one is, to show you how much worse off you might have been; the other, to remind you how much more wretched others are.

When I was a boy, I was consoled for cutting my finger by having my attention called to the fact that I had not broken my arm; and when I got a cinder in my eye, I was expected to feel more comfortable because my cousin had lost his by an accident.

The general opinion evidently is that the most agreeable consolation in sorrow is a contemplation of the greater misery of others; and the real ground of happiness is to know that others are suffering.

When a man in adversity complains of the demeanor of others toward him, inquire of his actions toward them.

Talk it over. "Pull not your hat about your brows." Seek a sympathetic companion and pour your sorrows into his kindly ears; not so much for the consolation he may administer, but because sad emotions assume their right proportions only when shown to others. In the darkened room of the mind they loom up like giants, when in the light they may prove to be pigmies. But hide your sorrows from the general gaze; sometimes the effort will conceal them from your own.

If we would only see it, there is a humorous side to nearly every occurrence; and if we did see it, what a preservative from despondency it would be!

Whatever happiness we get, we believe it is our own by right; when we miss that which we expected, we consider ourselves robbed. What impertinence! Does any one really pretend that because he wants something he is therefore entitled to it? Because he covets my house has he a fee in it? Suppose we give up for a while coveting and wanting, and settle down to doing and thinking and bearing. Perhaps that is the best way out, after all.

If you have no passions that you cannot conquer, you will have no griefs that you cannot bear.

The human body has a surprising ability to adapt its functions to the presence of permanent injuries and chronic maladies. Physicians call this the "tolerance of disease." The healthy mind has a similar power to recover its cheerfulness in the presence of an abiding grief or after an irreparable loss.

Indolence and Timidity are the jailers who rivet the fetters of Despondency. Courage and Activity will deliver us if we choose to summon them.

As the scars of battle are, in the opinion of the pious, proofs of the protection of Heaven, so a keen sense of past calamities testifies to a capacity for future enjoyment.

Between the leaves of the Book of Life why not press the violets, the lilies, and the roses which we find on our path, rather than the nettles and bitter weeds? We could then turn back its pages with satisfaction, and live again long-since-vanished joys.

There are few more accurate standards of a man's education, in the widest sense of the term, than the quality of the consolation he offers.

Would you learn the Universal Catholicon, the Balm for all wounds, the Panacea for all sorrows? I will whisper it: Work—hard physical work, arduous mental work. Try it; it will dry your tears, renew your love of life, recall the light of hope, and exorcise the evil spirits.

Strengthen the Will. If you have any earnest business in life, and are bound to carry it through, you will have no time for moping. If you have none, find some.

Look before and after. Do not allow the present to cheat you. The impression of the moment always claims more than it deserves, because we have not time to modify it by other thoughts and images. A present danger frightens us, though we may know it is infinitesimally small; a parting brings tears, though we are aware it is for the good of all; offensive words hurt us, though they may proceed from a contemptible person. Hasten to evoke memories and summon hopes which will beautify the incident, and strengthen the mind. Remember the slightness of the peril, speak of the happy return, recall the praise you have received from worthy lips.

The honey of life can be had only at the expense of some stings in its collection.

Whatever happens, take it as a matter of course. You are not running the world, nor born to set it right. You are not half so much the master of your own actions as you think you are.

Deal justly by yourself. Few do. They regret making that decision, or performing the other action, or neglecting such or such an opportunity. They reproach themselves for their hastiness or carelessness.

What folly! far worse results might have attended a different course. We can see but a very little way in life, and that very darkly. We can neither forecast events, nor predict our own decisions in new circumstances.

If we act at the time with reasonable prudence, we need never waste later moments in self-reproach. Any other decision than the one we adopted would likely enough have brought still more dismal consequences.

Remember that you are never deserted by all until you have deserted yourself.

Do not confound a decision with its results. The former may have been at the time the wisest possible, although the latter were disastrous.

What you consider a life-long mistake, your biographer may regard as the most fortunate decision of your life.

Grief lies in ambush. Its attack is like the spring of a lion. Its onset is the crisis that calls for the most heroic resistance. Despair seizes its victim in the first moments of a great sorrow.

Life is like a game of whist. Luck deals the cards, but we have the lead. We may receive a poor hand, but by playing it carefully win the odd.

Physical pain is an excellent antidote for mental pain. The hair shirt and the scourge were positive pleasures to the ascetic, because they distracted his thoughts from hell-fire.

The incivility of others is a frequent source of keen pain to sensitive dispositions. Socrates' advice was to look on an impolite person as on one deformed or repulsive in appearance; to be borne with when necessary, and fit to excite our pity rather than our anger. When some one asked Descartes how he met discourtesies he replied, "I try to live so high that they cannot reach me." The impoliteness of small children does not hurt our feelings; we should look on the uncivil generally with the same consciousness of our own superiority.

Grieve not at the ingratitude of others, even of your children. Much that looks like ingratitude is only forgetfulness. Again, what you think is a favor conferred, others may regard as a right respected. To some minds a sense of obligations received is really painful, and their ungrateful demeanor is an effort to escape this feeling. Perhaps you conferred the favor in a manner to induce such a feeling. When ingratitude pains you, overhaul your books and see if you find any debt of gratitude unpaid.

Do you seek consolation for the loss of a loved one? Call to mind, not the pleasant hours you passed together, but the kind actions, the proofs of affection, you received from him. Thus his personality will be idealized, and will become a sweet memory instead of a bitter regret.

I have repeatedly noticed, in my own life and in others, that the failure of a plan led to a success in another direction far greater than that anticipated from the original project. Two of the most eminent surgeons in the United States became physicians only in consequence of early failures in small business. When misfortunes happen, therefore, they may be paving the way for great successes. Our failure may be due to our superiority. Milton failed as a teacher of small boys, and Dr. Marion Sims as keeper of a country store. The Chipeways have a story of a man who could do no work, because he was so strong that he broke every tool he took up.

Are you vexed by some persistent anxiety, haunted by some ugly thought? Learn the secret, that the only way to stop thinking of anything is to think of something else. You cannot banish care by an effort of the will; but you can drive it away by changing the associations of your ideas, by engaging in some occupation which demands your constant and close attention.

Always keep in mind the uselessness of contending with the inflexible and inevitable processes of nature; but never let them become your masters when you can make them your servants.

Resignation is the more of a virtue the less it is exercised. A healthy tree bends before the blast, but straightens itself the moment the wind lulls. Resignation to evils that can be avoided is indolence or apathy.

When the world seems a desert to you and life a blank, reflect whether you have not had just such feelings before, and overlived them to enjoy happy days and smiling seasons.

Seek sympathy for your losses from a woman, for your failures from a man. A woman will not understand why you tried, if you failed.

Half of happiness is the recognition that we are happy; and half of misery is the forgetting how many causes of happiness we have.

Be sure you are more doleful than you need be. There is no liar like low spirits. Melancholy is a sort of mental stagnation; and stagnant pools are soon filled with foul growths.

You there, you on the verge of despair, sit down, take a pen, and write me off a list of your sorrows and misfortunes; and follow it with a faithful inventory of what you have left on the side of possible happiness, your faculties, your possessions, your friends and relatives, your acquirements, your tastes, your healthful activities, your probability of life, your reasonable expectations, not forgetting your duties to others and the gratification their fulfillment will give. Then I am ready to adjust the account.

Plato says that nothing in human life is worth much trouble; certainly many things give us more trouble than they are worth.

How small is your grief if you measure it by the standards of the universe! Look up at the calm and silent stars; they are billions of miles away. Notice that piece of sandstone; fifty million years have passed since the primeval tide washed its grains together. Is there not something in such thoughts that makes you a little ashamed of the preoccupation of your mind with its petty present cares?

Do you reflect sometimes that you are but one of fifteen hundred millions of human beings, fifty millions of whom die every year? Is it worth while passing your invisibly small share of life in worrying about trifles?

The only malady all covet is the only one which is absolutely fatal,—old age.

Death is the most and the least feared of any event. Seven of my most intimate friends committed suicide for various reasons, all good enough in their opinions. "No passion is so weak," remarks Bacon, "but that a little pushed it will master the fear of death."

The visits of death seem always inopportune. Dickens tells of a visit he paid to an Old Man's Home. He found that, in the opinion of the inmates, every old man died prematurely. They invariably said, "He brought it on hisself."

He who is haunted by the dread of dying makes himself miserable for fear he cannot make himself miserable longer.

When death is natural, that is, in extreme old age, it is neither feared nor felt. That it is so little a thing when natural, suggests that at all times we may deem it too great.

If we understood Death, we should no longer care for Life.

II. The Inseparable Connection of Pleasure and Pain.

The hard and strange lesson that I would teach in this chapter is, that dreams of unalloyed bliss are not merely fanciful, they are impossible of realization under any known conditions of life; that pleasure requires pain, joy demands sorrow, as the very condition of its existence; and that these pairs are inseparable twins, the presence of one being bound up in that of the other.

I here promulgate no new discovery in the science of mind, though it has been much overlooked by physiologists, and quite put one side by sanguine optimists in their rosy paintings of the future perfectibility and universal happiness of the human race. More than two thousand years ago Socrates dwelt upon this same uncanny blending of contraries. The jailer, as we are told in the "Phædo," of Plato, removed the galling iron fetters from the philosopher's ankles shortly before the cup of hemlock was handed him; and in this brief interval his friends gathered around him for the last farewell.

"And Socrates, sitting on the side of the bed, bent his leg and rubbed it with his hand, and in doing so said,—'How strange a thing, my friends, is that which is called Pleasure! and how oddly it is connected with what is called Pain! Pleasure and Pain do not come to man together; but if a person runs after the one and catches it, he almost immediately catches the other too, as if they were fastened together at one end. I think if Æsop had noticed this he would have compiled a fable to this effect: That the gods tried to reconcile these two opposites, and not being able to do this, fastened their extremities together so that when you take hold of one it pulls after it the other. And so it happens to me now; there was pain in my leg when the chain bound it, and now comes pleasure following the pain.'"

A law of physiology, a law of the whole universe, underlies these homely reflections of the ancient Greek.

On the one side, pleasure and pain are states of feeling totally opposed to each other both in sensation and in physical effect, pleasure being concomitant with an increase, pain with a decrease, of the vital functions; and yet, on the other, there is a unity, or, at any rate, a close analogy of action, under these contrary conditions of mental life. Each is a stimulus to new forms of mental change and biotic motion, though in the one instance the tendency of the new activity is toward a higher concentration of the individual life, and, in the other, toward its diminution or its disaggregation into other and lower forms.

A feeling of pleasure is an exaltation of sensation in some special set of nerves. These are stimulated to an unwonted exercise of their functions; but they can provide this disproportionate energy only by drafts on the general resources of the nervous system; and this must be paid back through exhaustion, fatigue, or, perhaps, actual pain.

A sensation of pain also demands for its presence special and unusual conditions of nervous activity, which also result in exhaustion of the powers of sensation, but, unfortunately, much later than in conditions of pleasure. Pain seems in some sort more our natural element, for we can bear it much longer than pleasure in equal degree. Generalizing on this fact, Schopenhauer reached the dismal conclusion—"The essential elements of all Life are pain and sorrow."

The mere cessation of pain is in itself a pleasure of considerable degree, as in the case of Socrates relieved from the chafing of his irons; indeed, probably some of the intensest moments of delight are those experienced on a sudden relief from acute suffering, or during the reaction from long privations.

It may not be quite correct to say that all pleasurable sensations are immediately derived from or directly lead to others of a painful character. There are some belonging to the organic life, such as the satisfaction of the desire for food or for muscular exercise, in which mere repose or remission is enough to repay the nervous drafts. But how close these are to pain is visible from the acuteness of the pangs of hunger, or the painfulness of prolonged positions of restraint.

Even exalted esthetic and intellectual pleasures, which seem to leave no sting behind and to require no goad for their advance, constantly make unfelt though heavy drafts on the nervous centres, the results of which, under the various forms of cerebral and spinal exhaustion and degeneration, physicians are obliged to take cognizance of only too often.

So close is the analogy between the two antagonistic sensations, that the one becomes merged into the other without our being able to mark the dividing line between them. A moderate pain may by its active diffusion actually bring a surplus of pleasure, as Professor Bain has remarked; and that an acute sensation of pleasure may pass into one of pain is matter of common observation. Thus, Pain is born of Pleasure, Pleasure of Pain; and memory and association have a tendency to diminish the extremes of each by recalling to the mind the sources from which it sprang. Some physiologists, therefore, refuse to discriminate between such inseparable feelings, and prefer to regard them both as manifestations of the same, calling it the "Pleasure-Pain sensation."

In all these respects what is true of these sensations also holds good of their analogues in the realm of emotions, as joy and sorrow, mirth and sadness, hope and fear, and the like. Each of these exercises, and by exercising exhausts, some fibres of the nervous system, and thus tends to develop its contrary.

The general law which, as far as it goes, explains these facts is that of the alternation or periodicity of the manifestations of force. This is the fundamental law of the Universe, beyond which no analysis has proceeded. Force, or Power, or Energy, wherever we discern it and under every one of its exhibitions, expresses itself in undulatory or rhythmical movements, pulsations of the primal potency, vibrations of the central harmony, of the universe. In the rise and fall of sensation and emotion the sequences of height and depth are as closely related as are the proportions of the crest and trough in the waves of the ocean, or those of the vibration of the strings of a musical instrument.

Such considerations as these, drawn from the unalterable laws of nature and life, show how short is the sight of those who look upon happiness as the uninterrupted continuance of pleasurable sensations, or would seek it in a ceaseless round of gayety. Far clearer was the vision of Pindar when he exclaimed, with the inspiration of a poet,—"Beneath every true pleasure hides the sense of a past pain." The dark background of sorrow can alone give full relief to the bright figure of joy. Grief is a part of gladness, and that life is not happy which has no unhappiness. So Browning, with characteristic insight and strength, puts in the mouth of one of his intensest characters,— "Naught is lacking to complete our bliss, but woe."

These are not mere paradoxes and literary refinements on scientific facts. All who have entered sympathetically into the deep and tender emotions of the human heart have felt and seen this mysterious and inseparable connection. It is so beautifully set forth in reference to one of the saddest griefs of life by Leigh Hunt, that I must quote his words. They are in his essay on the "Deaths of Little Children."

"Pain softens into pleasure as the darker hue of the rainbow melts into the brighter.... Made as we are, there are certain pains without which it would be difficult to conceive certain great and overbalancing pleasures. We may conceive it possible for beings to be made entirely happy; but in our composition, something of pain seems to be a necessary ingredient in order that the materials may turn to as fine an account as possible. The loss of children seems to be one of those necessary bitters thrown into the cup of humanity. If none at all ever took place, we should regard every little child as a man or a woman secured; and it will easily be conceived what a world of endearing cares and hopes this security would endanger. The very idea of infancy would lose continuity with us. Girls and boys would be future men and women, not present children. They would have attained their full growth in our imaginations, and might as well have been men and women at once. On the other hand, those who have lost an infant are never, as it were, without an infant child. They are the only persons who, in one sense, retain it always; and they furnish their neighbors with the same idea. The other children grow up to manhood or to womanhood and suffer all the changes of mortality. This one alone is rendered an immortal child. Death has arrested it with his kindly harshness, and blessed it into an eternal image of youth and innocence.

"Of such as these are the pleasantest shapes that visit our fancy and our hopes; they are the ever-smiling emblems of joy; the prettiest pages that wait upon imagination; lastly, 'Of these are the Kingdom of Heaven.'"

Something akin to the sweetness of these touching reflections is found in Sir Richard Steele's essay on "The Death of Friends," whose stately and gracious style seems ever treading a minuet at the court of good Queen Anne:—

"When we are advanced in years, there is not a more pleasing entertainment than to recollect the many we have parted with that have been dear to us.... It is necessary to revive the old places of grief in our memory, to lead the mind unto that sobriety of thought which poises the heart and makes it beat with due time, without being quickened by desire or retarded by despair from its proper and equal motion."

Thus it is that sadness is ofttimes a necessary and the best preparative for gladness. The blacker the shadow, the brighter is the light that casts it. In all pleasurable feelings there must be the alternations from exercise to remission and repose; and in proportion as such feelings are keen, will pain take the place of simple exhaustion. When the waves of emotion are but ripples on the surface of life, stirred by the zephyrs of light desires, the remission will be but a passing sense of fatigue; but when the sensitive heart is shaken to its depths by the mighty winds of passion, then the reaction will be not less profound, and the moments of wild joy will be repaid to the uttermost by periods of dejection and despair. In such temperaments there is danger of the morbid persistence of the period of depression, and ready recourse must be had to diversion and occupation to avoid this considerable peril.

There is a singular but comforting contrast in the influence of time on pleasure and pain and the mental states which correspond to them.

Through repetition and habitual exercise we may become passionately fond of what at first was painful or disgusting. Witness the use of tobacco and all other so-called "acquired tastes." The physician becomes enamored of the studies of the hospital ward and the dissecting room; persons who are at first sight repulsive become tolerable and then companionable; studies which we take up with dislike later on fascinate us.

How different with pleasures! Their tendency is not upward but downward, gravitating ever toward the lower and painful strata of sensation. Those built on a foundation of previous pain alone escape a merely evanescent existence. How quickly facile loves are sated! Ennui arrives never earlier than when enjoyment is gratuitous. The law, alas, holds good even for our dearest joys; as Mrs. Browning wrote:—

"Entertain

Your best and gladdest thoughts but long enough,

And they will all prove sad enough to sting."

Time, transmuter of all things, turns delight into disgust, and aversion into love, but his metamorphoses constantly warn us that permanence is related to painfulness and duration depends on endurance.

Pain is more natural to us than pleasure. We bear it better. Bad fortune is easier sustained than good. The hour of prosperity is more trying than that of adversity. These are commonplaces, and speak for the universal recognition of this feature of mind.

Our first language is wailing, and our most hilarious laughter brings tears.

Do you say that had the Creative Hand been yours, pain would not have been in the world? Compel my belief in your words by seeing you relieve all pain now in your power to relieve.

The abrupt ending of any deep emotion is unpleasant, even though a sad one. When we have been sailing in the clouds, the descent to earth is always a shock.

Any action, however trifling, assumes an immeasurable significance when we know it is performed for the last time. It evokes the idea of the Irrevocable and the Infinite, of Death and Destiny. Our souls hear the distant dirge, *Vale, vale, eternumque vale.*

We can always explain our merriment, but often not our melancholy. Glee is concrete and affirmative; dejection is vague and negative; and the negative is unlimited.

The drama of life is a tragedy, for its last scene is always that of the death of the title-role. We take the greatest interest in the spectacle, but rarely care to remember the denouement.

If you love life so much, why complain of ennui? There is nothing like it for lengthening the hours, and thus giving you longer to live.

The more pleasant the moments, the swifter they fly. Perfect happiness would destroy Time.

Many pleasures, like Barbary figs, are gathered at the cost of bleeding fingers.

III. The Education of Suffering.

What is suffering? What is sorrow?

Nought but the wounds in our conflict with the imperfections and limitations of life, with the elements of death and annihilation, with the powers of falsehood and hatred. The inappeasable thirst in the human heart for the fullness of existence, for complete happiness, could only be satisfied with all love and all truth, and we should need the term of all time in which to attain them.

Pain and grief are, therefore, evident proofs of the capacity for broader conditions of being; and at the same time they are the guides, pointing out what to avoid and what to seek, in order to attain this end of all desire.

This is true of all organic existence; but man alone is capable of Sorrow, a passion allied to the most exalted moods of mind, presenting to it the image of infinity, defining and educating his desires by the clear exhibition of their painful limitations, and thus revealing to his perceptions new though arduous paths, which will lead him to a loftier evolution and broader horizons.

He finds that sorrow is an initiation into the hidden mysteries of life. Through its draped portals he enters the Temple of Sadness, there to learn "the elder truths, and the secrets that cannot be spoken." He must be bathed in the fountain of tears and be branded with the blade of adversity before he is established in the novitiate of the order of Our Mother of Sorrows.

Once admitted to her chosen band, he looks back without regret at his earlier and placid joys. His sorrow lives on within him as a new and indestructible force of character, expressing itself in added strength of will, clearness of perception, and breadth of sympathies. It has imparted to life another meaning, one more male and heroic, and yet tender, such as no pleasures can suggest or beget. The years may be paler, their flowers fewer, their grave-mounds more numerously strewn across his pathway; over them he steps with steady tread, his eye fixed on the work which he has learned is for him to do, asking neither about its rewards nor its results.

This is the spirit of those teachers and lovers of their kind, who have taken as their own the sorrows of the race; it is the spirit of those martyrs to liberty who have fallen to free their country from the yoke of tyrants; and of those sufferers for truth's sake who have been tortured and burned by the Churches rather than live by lying recantations.

History constantly proves that the worthiest prizes of life, its loftiest virtues, and its most ennobling ambitions, are sold only at the price of suffering. The great world-religions, Buddhism and Christianity, began with proclaiming this final fact of life; and to its instinctive recognition by the experience of all mankind are due their conquests over the faiths which held out the allurements of material success and physical pleasure. The spirit of Christianity is the spirit of sadness. To it the house of mourning is ever better than the house of mirth. The Cross is the symbol of suffering; the steps are blood-stained that mount to Calvary; anguish and death are at its summit; for suffering and death are the signs, the admonitions, and the entrance to the Infinite.

Art acknowledges the same inspirations as its highest. Sad emotions attract most potently because they arise from the unplumbed depth of the soul, and suggest its limitless dimensions. They attest the words of the poet, that "Man's grief is but his grandeur in disguise." There is always a strange attraction about scenes of suffering; the appetite is always keen "to sup full of horrors;" our emotions are more profoundly stirred by the spectacle of pain and anguish than by that of any imaginable pleasure.

Therefore the works as well as the lives of great artists have been full of sadness. The group of the Laocoon struggling in the deadly coil of the serpent; the agony of the crucifixion; the tragedies of love and jealousy and devotion,—these have been the chosen themes of painters, sculptors and dramatists; chosen because they mark graphically the struggles of our common nature with its limits, ennobled by its ambition to leap beyond them.

Every soul knows, unconsciously and instinctively, that sorrow is the only teacher of what is most valuable in life. It alone develops fortitude, and therefore it commands the respect of all; it alone teaches sympathy, and therefore it enlists the admiration of all. No character is ripe which has not crispened under its sharp breath; none is of finest temper but those forged by its heavy blows. The noblest lives are sad; but those who have quaffed the severe joy of sorrow care little for the light froth of pleasure.

The quality of high energy is developed only by affliction. Wrestling with it, the sinews of the mind are trained. We must go forth and seek new supports in life, when we have lost those which we loved and depended upon. By such an effort, we reconcile ourselves to the loss, gain a victory over fate, strengthen our minds, and reach an air of wider freedom. The blast may beat at the gate, but all is quiet within. There is a habit of sadness which is not gloomy, which may share and admire the delights of life, but which is ever ready to meet the storms of misfortune with serenity and fortitude. Such a habit of mind lifts one above the threats and disturbances of the ceaseless struggle for existence into the companionship of ideas and powers which the poet rightly calls celestial:—

"Wer nicht sein Brod mit Thränen ass,

Wer nicht die kummervollen Nächte

Auf seinem Lager weinend sass,

Der kennt euch nicht, ihr himmlischen Mächte."

There is a ministry of grief, a compensation in calamity, a remedial property in misfortune, sweet uses in adversity, which need but to be recognized and cherished for the sting to be blunted, and what seems at first a grief without an element of alleviation, to become in time the foundation of a higher happiness. How often may one exclaim with Cleopatra, in the midst of her immeasurable losses:—

"My desolation,

Does begin to make a better life."

We need occasionally some violent and painful shock to waken us from the lethargy of pleasant custom, to break the shackles of agreeable and enervating habit, to tear us by the roots from the soil in which we lazily vegetate, and transplant us into fresh and richer fields. The beautiful elements in a noble character are woven together by the experience of afflictions, as the pearls which form the design of a brooch are held in place by the thread of iron on which they are strung.

The affections which are deep and pure leave behind them when they are severed by fate a happiness which is comparable to that of their enjoyment. Our sorrow for such is accompanied with an inexpressible sense of consolation, the firm and sweet assurance—"'Tis better to have loved and lost, than never to have loved at all."

This compensation flows, from the nature of affection itself, because it is essentially unselfish, and ever seeking objects outside the circle of egoistic instincts. It is Love that teaches us that Joy and Sorrow are twins; and at the same time sharply defines what are the true objects of affection. Its sweet waters pour inexhaustible streams of consolation for the wounds of Fate, but not for those of Fortune. For the loss of money or rank or other mere externality it offers no such assuagement, for it deems all such losses beneath its sovereign notice. The solace for these must be sought in fortitude and courage and resignation. Only of the loss of such lower means of happiness as these is the saying of the poet true, that "A sorrow's crown of sorrows is remembering happier things." Rather let us say, the only sorrows we should not be ashamed of, are those which turn into joy. The griefs that embitter and harden, follow loves that are lowering.

Noble sorrow is the teacher of sympathy. The sense or the memory of our own pain awakens the desire to relieve the pain of others. Compassion and Pity are the offspring of grief. It also teaches tolerance, charity for the imperfections of others, and a knowledge of the limitations and deficiencies of our common nature, without which knowledge the successful endeavor for any of the higher aims of existence is not possible. The sense of physical suffering has been the guiding principle in the evolution of organic forms from the monad up to man. His future and higher evolution, that of his spirit-powers, will come from his mental suffering and the lessons he will draw from it.

Thus, at the end of our wide wandering in pursuit of Happiness, we look back and see that it is absent from nothing in life, not even from pain and sorrow; nay, that when all else has gone, when youth and health and fortune and love have left us, when we look forward despairingly to nought but loneliness and suffering, our very despair may prove to be divine, "begotten by the finite upon the infinite," and from its depths we may draw a rapture unknown to common pleasures, and taste the sweet waters of a bliss which is celestial.

Who would wish to escape suffering himself, when suffering makes up so large a part of the experiences of his fellow men? Who would seek by any base flight to avoid Sorrow, when Sorrow alone can teach him the highest meaning of Life?

History is ever ready to point out how nations have been benefited by calamities, and churches by persecutions. Why not believe that the same rule holds good in our own lives?

Think what we should miss if all went smoothly with us! Without pain, we should not know pity; without danger, we should not develop courage; without receiving injuries, no chance to show forgiveness; without affliction, no opportunity for fortitude; without ingratitude, no means of proving disinterestedness; without injustice, no occasion for forbearance; without violence, no training in self-control. Really, it seems that to encounter misfortunes must be the finest fortune in life!

The surgeon restores a stiffened joint or an atrophied muscle by painful manipulations. Nothing but painful experiences will restore a sluggish mind to activity and enjoyment.

To forget even for a short time those we have loved and lost seems a lack of fealty to them; but if their influence is ever present with us to our good, our joy is a worthier memorial to them than would be endless repining.

The memory of a great sorrow obliterates the slight asperities of daily life.

The mingling of tears is a transfusion of spirit. A sorrow in common is the strongest of covenants.

The only complete satisfaction of the sense of living is its sacrifice.

The sweetest joys are consoled sorrows.

☺ ☺ ☺

Printed by Libri Plureos GmbH in Hamburg,
Germany